The Big Green Poetry Machine

North West England Poets

Edited by Annabel Cook

First published in Great Britain in 2009 by:

Young Writers

Young Writers
Remus House
Coltsfoot Drive
Peterborough
PE2 9JX
Telephone: 01733 890066
Website: www.youngwriters.co.uk

Book Design by Spencer Hart & Tim Christian

SB ISBN 978-1-84431-001-7

Foreword

Young Writers' Big Green Poetry Machine is a showcase for our nation's most brilliant young poets to share their thoughts, hopes and fears for the planet they call home.

Young Writers was established in 1991 to nurture creativity in our children and young adults, to give them an interest in poetry and an outlet to express themselves. Seeing their work in print will encourage them to keep writing as they grow, and become our poets of tomorrow.

Selecting the poems has been challenging and immensely rewarding. The effort and imagination invested by these young writers makes their poems a pleasure to enjoy reading time and time again.

Contents

Linacre Primary School, Bootle

Marlfields Primary School, Congleton

Milnrow Parish CE Primary School, Milnrow

Netherton Moss Primary School, Netherton

Our Lady's RC Primary School, Aspull

Prospect Vale Primary School, Cheadle

SS Aidan & Oswald RC Primary School, Royton

St John's CE Primary School, Heaton Mersey

The Poems

The War

The war is bad,
It always turns out sad,
We always get a fright,
When we see it in sight.

Everyone is crying,
People are dying,
Mothers, fathers, sisters, brothers,
Are suffering as well as others.

They can't survive,
People losing their lives,
There is lots and lots of death,
People taking their last breath.

We can't wait anymore,
We'll have to stop the war!

Muhammad Hashim & Saffran Khan (9)
Alma Park Primary School, Levenshulme

Do Your Bit

Recycle your tins and your cans,
And do your bit for the lands.
Don't litter, don't waste things,
Our world will go up in springs.
Please don't throw your cigarettes,
Other people are at threat.

Our furry friends are becoming extinct,
And we don't want that, do we?
And when we throw our plastic bags
They flow into the sea.
Save the world
Save the world
Do our bit for the land.

Kike-Lomo Adenowo (10)
Alma Park Primary School, Levenshulme

Rainforest

So many trees being cut down,
Help the rainforest all around,
Some people don't give a care,
Trees give us oxygen and air,
Stop killing the trees,
Make sure you save the trees,
It'll change the climate,
We can't survive without it.
There are lots of floods,
And droughts and things,
Everyone is dying,
So please help the rainforest!

Aisha & Sharise Smith (9)
Alma Park Primary School, Levenshulme

Helping The Environment

Stop, stop, stop pollution,
Let's have a revolution,
The Earth is gonna be hot, hot, hot,
Don't put it in a dangerous spot, spot, spot.

Pollution is bad,
So don't make the Earth sad,
In Africa no water there will be
In other countries too much of water you will see.
Stop pollution! Have a revolution! Stop pollution!
Find a solution.

Abdul Azeez Morafa & Haroon Wahid (9)
Alma Park Primary School, Levenshulme

Pollution And Energy

The light is always on,
But soon that will be gone.
We must not waste energy,
Then we will be able to see.

In a car don't go,
Walk like a star, just so.
Just be good,
Like you should and walk!

Farhana Begum (9)
Alma Park Primary School, Levenshulme

War

Think about the people,
What they're going through.
Many people dying,
What are we to do?
Stop the killing,
Stop the corruption.
Stop, stop, stop,
The destruction.

Luke Cox (9) & Qasim (10)
Alma Park Primary School, Levenshulme

Try To Recycle

Recycle your tins and cans
And pick up any litter you see
You'll find it very hard
Then we'll be free, from misery.

Chontay Kovrac-Richards & Asraa (10)
Alma Park Primary School, Levenshulme

Charity Helps!

Charity is a time when you give
It will really help.
You'll feel how it makes a change to the world around you.
It will really help.
So please give, it will really help.
It will help the elderly and the poor.
So please give more.

Zara Choudhury (9)
Alma Park Primary School, Levenshulme

Litterers

Start throwing it in the bin,
Dropping rubbish is a sin,
And if you throw it on the floor,
You will have to pay for sure.
It makes the place a mess
The people will be depressed.

Qasim, Rakshan & Ali Zia (9)
Alma Park Primary School, Levenshulme

Turn Off The Electricity

Turn off the lights,
Turn off the computers.
Don't waste electricity
Remember to turn off the electricity in your house.

Chelsea Burgess (10)
Alma Park Primary School, Levenshulme

I Am Sad

I am sad because you poison our water supply.
I am sad we beg for food.
I am sad you kill our fish.
I am sad you are killing me.
I am sad you kill people.
I am sad you kill our world.
I am sad you just don't look at me.
I am sad because you poison our water.
I am sad you kill my family.
I am sad you burnt our crops.
I am sad you made me sad.
I am sad so much.
I am sad you closed the sea.
I am sad you are killing me.
I am so sad.
I am sad you made the animals die.
I am sad you took my food.
I am so, so sad! Help me.
I am sad so much, help, help me.
I am sad you made us beg for food.
I am sad, so sad.
I am sad you made me so sad.
I am sad you don't help.
I am sad, so sad.
I am sad, so, so sad.

Libby Harrison (9)
Cadishead Primary School, Cadishead

It Was Awful

It was awful
The beach is closed because of pollution
It was awful
Recycle don't throw bottles and glass away
It was awful
Care for the world because the world's dying
It was awful
People have to wear masks from the smoke and oil
It was awful
The fish are dying because of oil
It was awful
The fire is blocking the light
It was awful
They have to dig a big hole to put the rubbish in
It was awful
The smoke is in the air
It was awful
The buildings are getting burnt down
It was awful
Our world is dying and everyone is crying
It was awful
Can you not dig a big hole
It was awful.

Lewis Jordan (10)
Cadishead Primary School, Cadishead

Endangered Animals

Endangered animals
What can we do to help them?
The woods are being chopped down,
But animals need a home to live in.
How can we save nature?
Just think of all the animals without a home.

Ellie Kaye (8)
Cadishead Primary School, Cadishead

Poor People

Some people are fat
Some people are thin
Sometimes they look like a rubbish bin.
They can be big, sometimes small,
And none of them will grow nice and tall.
Sometimes they are skinny
And some may be mini.
No matter what we do
We need to help them too.
Please don't let go
Because we need to help them.
Now it's up to you
Do your best
And never forget
To give food
To the poor.

Sasha Hoffman (8)
Cadishead Primary School, Cadishead

Poor People

Poor people
Poor people are in danger
So let them have some money
So they can have a teacher
And they can play and learn a different way
And we should pay
To help the environment today
And to help the poor people
And help them fast
I am sorry for the poor
Let's help them with the war
And save the world from global warming.

Marc Robinson (8)
Cadishead Primary School, Cadishead

Recycling

Recycling, recycling
What can we do to help the world to recycle?
We can recycle paper.
We can recycle banana peel.
We can recycle bottles.
So please, please, keep recycling
Because the world needs to recycle.

Sometimes we forget to recycle.
But we have to recycle every day.
If we didn't recycle the world would be full of rubbish.
We can recycle fast.
If we recycle we help the environment.
We don't want rubbish on the floor.

Anais Highton (8)
Cadishead Primary School, Cadishead

I Was Angry!

You took my fish
I was angry!
You took my food supplies
I was angry!
My family and friends are dying
I was angry!
Please give the food back!
I was angry!
I'm very ill
I was angry!
Give £2 a month
You could save a life of a young child.

Melissa Taylor (9)
Cadishead Primary School, Cadishead

Litter

This place is a dump, we want to make it clean, so clear it up.
Do not fuss or you are a scruff.
Clear it up, make it clean, otherwise you are mean.
The dump is getting bigger, so take away all the litter.
Crisp packets flying in the sky with the wind.
Cans which should be binned.
Dumping litter on the floor more and more.
We can all clear up this dump even if it's hard.
We can get rid of it.
If there is sticky stuff on the floor,
You will be getting insects on the floor.
Instead of litter being on the floor, we can recycle more and more.

Riya Kotecha (7)
Cadishead Primary School, Cadishead

Untitled

We're blocking the right
The Earth is dying, it's a disgrace

We're blocking the right
It's a disgrace and it's in my face

We're blocking the right
You're poisoning our water supplies

We're blocking the right
You're killing the world

We're blocking the right
The animals are dying.

Dale Lowndes-Smith (9)
Cadishead Primary School, Cadishead

I Was Angry . . .

I was angry . . .
Fish died.
I was angry . . .
You poisoned my fish.
I was angry . . .
Then you're taking my fish.
I was angry . . .
You wanted to kill them.
I was angry . . .
Cars killed my fish because of toxins.
I was angry . . .

Ethan Hall (9)
Cadishead Primary School, Cadishead

The Recycling Robot

The recycling robot's on his way
What have you recycled today?
Tin cans, bottles, paper and plastic,
Let's recycle, it's fantastic!

The recycling robot's on his way
Helping save the world every day,
All the rubbish we throw out
Gets recycled when he's about.

The recycling robot's here to stay
Helping us to recycle every day.

Sam Glossop (8)
Cadishead Primary School, Cadishead

Be Eco-Friendly!

Everything is really dull
Gas in the air is really full.

Stop throwing litter
Don't be bitter.

Save the world, walk to school,
Don't get in the car,
Instead walk on the tar.

What a disgrace it's near my place,
The litter is in my face.

Mollie Anne Moreton (10)
Cadishead Primary School, Cadishead

Recycling

Recycling every day is what we do.
We need to help the poor people too.
I've found litter here and there,
I've found litter everywhere.
Some litter is big,
Some litter is small,
But who cares we have got to help them all.
It might be easy,
It might be hard,
But we've got to tidy up the yard.

Eden Horsfall (8)
Cadishead Primary School, Cadishead

I Was Angry

I was angry . . . you took my fish.
I was angry . . . you took my food.
I was angry . . . my family is dying.
I was angry . . . my friends are dying.
I was angry . . . please give my family back!
I was angry . . . please give the fish back!
I was angry . . . please give four pounds
I was angry . . . you put oil in my water to kill them all
I was angry . . . they were very ill.

Tiegan Lilly Gillon (10)
Cadishead Primary School, Cadishead

Recycling

Rubbish everywhere.
How can we share?
Rubbish everywhere,
Over streets and tips.
Bits, pieces, things that shouldn't be there,
Like cardboard and bottles that we can recycle.
Recycling is fun, have a go
It is fun, have a go.

Alex Chen (8)
Cadishead Primary School, Cadishead

Untitled

We have found litter on the ground.
We pick up litter off the ground.
We don't like litter on the ground.
That's why we pick it up.
I know why it is because we don't like litter on the ground.

Holly Fay (7)
Cadishead Primary School, Cadishead

Diseased

The Earth is diseased
The fish are diseased in pollution
The Earth is diseased
You're dumping in the lake
The Earth is diseased
It's a disgrace
The Earth is diseased
Be green!

Samuel Platt (9)
Cadishead Primary School, Cadishead

Beach

We are aware the pollution is high
The animals are going to die
Stop using your car
You may as well walk on the tar
It really is a disgrace
We deserve to live in a better place
You have closed the beach
And then I heard a screech.

Abby Woodward (9)
Cadishead Primary School, Cadishead

Recycling

We can recycle lots of things,
Paper, rubbish, banana skins, plastic bottles
And soil and leaves all can be recycled.
Recycling helps our world, we all need to do it.
My family does some recycling
Do you?
We all need to do more recycling.
Do you?

Imogen Lynch (7)
Cadishead Primary School, Cadishead

Stop Killing Me

Your rubbish is going into the ocean
Stop killing me.
The world is disgraceful,
Stop killing me.
The gas is toxic,
Stop killing me.
I can't breathe, I'm choking.
Stop killing me.

Julie Helps (9)
Cadishead Primary School, Cadishead

Recycling

Rubbish here, rubbish there, I see rubbish everywhere.
People drop litter, they just don't care,
It's not my job, we've got to share.
If we don't recycle, the world will be a tip.
It won't be very pleasant.
We could save the world by recycling
So get up, don't be lazy,
Don't just dump, we could save our planet today.

Samuel Roberts (8)
Cadishead Primary School, Cadishead

Untitled

If you go out in the smoke
Remember everybody starts to choke
So you will need a drink of Coke
Then you see a bloke
Dying in smoke
People can't have a joke
So remember to recycle
But always keep your bicycle.

Cameron McGloin (10)
Cadishead Primary School, Cadishead

Electricity

Save electricity
When you're not watching TV switch it off by the plug
Then the world shall have no electricity bills
But it's not just the TV
You should switch off things like a computer
Game Boy, remote control car and so many others.

Henry Samuel Wright (7)
Cherry Tree Primary School, Lymm

Eco Rap!

I am an eco dude,
I even grow my own food,
Fruit and veg that's the key,
There'll be enough food for my tea,
I take my own bags to the shop,
And I always recycle empty bottles of pop,
Recycle paper, save a tree,
There'll be enough oxygen for me,
Don't take the car, if you're not going far,
Why not use your bike or go for a hike?
Pollution, pollution makes me sad,
It chokes the Earth and that is bad.
I do not waste electricity, I always turn off my TV.
The world is dying, and I am trying
To convince you to be eco too!

Rebecca Walker (10)
Cherry Tree Primary School, Lymm

Make The World A Better Place

How can we make the world a better place?
Cycle or walk, don't use the car,
If you're not going very far.
It will make you a lot, lot fitter,
And while I'm at it, don't drop litter.
Wrappers and cans all over the floor,
I just can't stand it anymore!
Help keep the world clean and green
People who don't will soon be seen!
Find a place for rubbish to go
Search everywhere high and low
That's how we can make the world a better place!

Alex Lee (9)
Cherry Tree Primary School, Lymm

Save The Planet

Try to make the world a better place.
Switch off lights,
Pull out plugs.
Help the world
With all its stuff.
Turn off TVs when they're not used.
Turn off radios so they don't blast in other rooms.
Try to walk, don't use the car,
Because when you walk or use your bike,
You will get just as far.
Each little thing everyone does,
Makes a big change to all of us.

Tia Wilkinson (7)
Cherry Tree Primary School, Lymm

Saving Electricity

E lectricity, electricity
L ights up our houses and brightens up our nights
E lectricity, electricity
C an we do without it?
T urn it off!
R emember
I n our homes and factories
C an we do without it?
I n our shops and offices
T urn it off!
Y ou must all do your bit to switch it off.

Savannah Williamson (8)
Cherry Tree Primary School, Lymm

Recycling

Recycle, recycle
Cans and tins,
Recycle, recycle
Use your blue bins,
Cardboard, paper, plastic and glass
Use them again and make them last.
Just look at the great big landfill sites
Where rubbish is rotting day and night,
Do not litter, do not waste
The world would be a cleaner place.

Eve Lundstram (7)
Cherry Tree Primary School, Lymm

Recycle

Recycle, recycle
Pick up rubbish
Recycle, recycle
Don't put paper or cardboard in the bin.
Just recycle otherwise it's too late.
Recycle, recycle
Recycle it all.
Recycle, recycle,
It will make a difference to our world.
Recycle, recycle.

Rebecca Layhe (7)
Cherry Tree Primary School, Lymm

Saving The Rainforest

R ainforests keep them clean
A nd most of all don't cut down the trees
I n the wild animals are hurt
N ow even trees can make us a shirt
F riendly, they're very friendly in a way
O verall they're for us every day
R unny raindrops falling off them
E njoying it and having lots of fun
S tarting to dry, the trees are getting cold
T omorrow it will be another day for them to be old.

Robyn Lees (8)
Cherry Tree Primary School, Lymm

Extinction

E very animal is precious to us
eX plain why we are not making a fuss
T each our children how to care
I t's very important we are fair
N obody's caring anymore
C onstantly fighting and causing war
T igers and pandas are trying to survive
I t's very hard for them to stay alive
O nly with our help will they see
N othing should stop them from being free.

Marc Harrison (9)
Cherry Tree Primary School, Lymm

Pollution!

Dump the car, it's not far
Get the bus, save the car
Air pollution is a problem in our days
Look up in the sky, aeroplanes going by
Let's go abroad less and less
Great Britain would be the best
Let's say stop to this pollution
And find a suitable solution
This could be world's end
Let it not become a trend!

Mia Stubbs (10)
Cherry Tree Primary School, Lymm

Stop Pollution

Don't throw rubbish in the river
Forget putting oil in the sea
Make the world a better place
To be known across the Milky Way
Let's stop pollution, let's find a solution!
The world is getting infected,
Getting infected badly,
It's time to make the world better,
Together we will try hard,
Let's stop pollution, let's find a solution.

Harvey Metcalf (8)
Cherry Tree Primary School, Lymm

Recycling

R ecycle your tins!
E veryone puts them into their blue bins!
C ycle to your nearest park!
Y ou'd use a submarine to meet a shark!
C rystal blue, shiny sea!
L eave some time to let it free!
I f you want to ride a bike!
N ever avoid to take a hike!
G o out tonight, but instead of going in a car,
ride a bike or walk!

Toby Boston (9)
Cherry Tree Primary School, Lymm

Pollution

P ilots flying every day
O n the road is where you stay
L ots of fumes in the air
L ots of you will stop and stare
U and me can make a change
T he result will be quite strange
I nstead you could walk
O n the way you could stop and talk
N ow we need you! Walk and help the world.

Kathryn Morris (9)
Cherry Tree Primary School, Lymm

War

W ar machines, blowing up streets, killing people,
A ir raid sirens screaming, screeching, noise as loud as thunder.
R unning, shouting, people hiding in their homes.

Eddie Swinney (8)
Cherry Tree Primary School, Lymm

Litter, Litter

Litter, litter,
Makes the world sad.
Make it glad.
Litter, litter,
All over the floor.
Make sure there is no more.
Litter, litter,
Make the world safe,
Make it a better place.

Ollie McFerran (7)
Cherry Tree Primary School, Lymm

Extinction

The animals were watching
Who was going to come?
It was exciting and it was fun.
The animals all played a game,
They had to guess someone's name.
'I will guess, panda,' the dinosaur said.
'Or elephant,' said the dodo nodding his head.
'Oh,' said the mammoth, 'let me think,
Who will be next to be extinct?'

Alex Longshaw (7)
Cherry Tree Primary School, Lymm

Recycling

R ecycling paper keeps us cool
E veryone needs to so you're not a fool
C ollecting cans will save our world
Y ou keep recycling the Earth will stay curled
C an't we keep the Earth clean?
L itter can be recycled to something that gleams
I ncredible bins can be recycled into tins
N aughty rubbish can be recycled into more bins
G et into business and make a change.

Christopher George Percival (9)
Cherry Tree Primary School, Lymm

Recycling

Recycle, recycle
Cans and tins
It's good for the world
And use recycle bins
Save them, save them
Paper and glass
Cardboard and plastic bottles
Just do it like that.
Reuse, reuse.

Caitlin Sheron (7)
Cherry Tree Primary School, Lymm

The Litter-Pick

I went on a litter-pick,
Around the village where I'm from,
It was fun, I enjoyed it,
Before it looked like a bomb!

Someone found pyjamas,
I found stripy socks to go on your feet,
A five pound note and Coke cans
We enjoyed cleaning up the street!

Zoe Phillips (10)
Cherry Tree Primary School, Lymm

Recycle And Reuse

Recycle, recycle,
It's good for the planet,
Use blue bins for tins and bags,
Put plastic in recycling bins.

Reuse, reuse
As much as you can.
If you reuse you can save trees,
If you reuse you can turn a bean can into a pencil pot.

Dylan Boston (7)
Cherry Tree Primary School, Lymm

Endangered Animals

Tigers, tigers,
They're endangered
We're running out of them
So help them live.
Elephants, elephants
They're endangered
There's only a few left
Oh poor elephants, help them live.

Georgina Powell (8)
Cherry Tree Primary School, Lymm

Rainforests Are Dying

Rainforests are dying
Animals are crying
Their homes are being taken
Their lives are being shaken
Trees are like gold
Even if they're old
So give them a helping hand
And let them stand!

Pavan Sidhu (9)
Cherry Tree Primary School, Lymm

Recycling

Recycle, recycle,
It's good for the world.
Recycle plastic bottles and glass bottles too.
Think of the landfill sites, they're full of junk and rotten glass.
Recycle plastic bottles by using them again and again.
Ignore the landfill sites, recycle instead.

Olivia Cook (7)
Cherry Tree Primary School, Lymm

Recycle, Recycle

It is good for the planet
Save cans, glass and paper.
Don't throw paper, cans and glass in the bin.
Reduce, reduce
Reuse as much as you can.
Save trees and plastic
Also save cardboard.
Recycle, recycle.

Matthew Mason (7)
Cherry Tree Primary School, Lymm

Litterbugs

Litter, litter, put it in the bin
If you throw it on the floor that's a sin
Litter, litter, get off my street
Keep it tidy, keep it neat
Litter, litter, you make me sad
Litter, litter, go away
And don't come back
That is what I can say!

Rahul Sidhu (8)
Cherry Tree Primary School, Lymm

Animals In Danger

A nimals in danger with nothing to eat
N obody even gives them a treat
I n the jungle they are frightened
M an cutting trees, rainforests getting tightened
A nimals, animals, where will you go?
L eave them alone - let their numbers grow!

Robert Tilling (9)
Cherry Tree Primary School, Lymm

Litter

Litter, litter, everywhere
People really do not care
Wrappers of chocolate bars
Thrown out of cars
Fast food cartons at our feet
Plastic bags blown down the street
Litter, litter everywhere
People really do not care.

Maya Skye Anstee (8)
Cherry Tree Primary School, Lymm

Recycling

Recycle, recycle
Put plastic tins in recycling bins.
Don't make the world bad, make it glad.
If you save paper, you save trees.
Reduce, reduce
Stop the litter abuse,
Save seas, save skies,
Make the world a better place.

Chris Mundy (7)
Cherry Tree Primary School, Lymm

Litterbugs

L itter, litter, litterbugs
I wish you would go away
T he Earth would be a much nicer place if you
T hought about your actions,
E ven if it's a plastic bag,
R emember to tidy up the world!

Anna Dempsey (8)
Cherry Tree Primary School, Lymm

The War

People starving, not much food
If they found it, they chewed and chewed
Lots of people getting shot
If they stood there you would rot
Many people walking around
Except planes, not much sound
Lots of people on the street
Kill your friends to get some meat.

James Pitcher (9)
Cherry Tree Primary School, Lymm

Recycle

R euse containers that things come in
E veryone can recycle, just don't use the bin
C an you find a solution?
Y ou can help to stop pollution
C an't you recycle everywhere?
L ook around, it's unclean air
E veryone can recycle, now you can make a difference.

Rachel Smith (9)
Cherry Tree Primary School, Lymm

Recycle

R ecycling is the thing to do
E arth needs your help and people do too
C ans and bottles can be recycled
Y ou can't keep wasting precious land
C an't keep polluting our fresh air
L ights and lamps, turn them off!
E verybody do your bit.

Callum Charles Lee Frazer (8)
Cherry Tree Primary School, Lymm

Rubbish

R ubbish is cluttering up the world
U nder bushes, in the streets
B ottles, cans under our feet
B eing careful with our waste
I s the right thing to do
S ave our planet for us all
H elp others heed our call.

Sophie McKenzie (8)
Cherry Tree Primary School, Lymm

Recycle

R educe waste
E verybody needs to do their bit
C ans, bottles and glass
Y ou know what to do
C arry your rubbish to your recycle bin
L et's make a change today
E njoy recycling.

Nicole Westley (8)
Cherry Tree Primary School, Lymm

Disease

D irty water making people die
I t is time to make a try
S ome people are dying around the Earth
E veryone is sometimes diseased from birth
A nd everyone is trying to help
S ome people don't have good health
E veryone should work together to make it right.

Mitchell Dolman (9)
Cherry Tree Primary School, Lymm

Recycling

R ecycling paper is very good
E ven cardboard will stop the flood
C an you recycle a lot more?
Y ou can help stop ruin our floor
C an you put rubbish in the bin?
L ots of people put them on a tin
E veryone knows how to recycle.

Samuel Luke Sheron (9)
Cherry Tree Primary School, Lymm

Animals In Danger

A nimals are in danger
N ever forget it is major
I n the forest they live
M eat and weeds we give
A lot of us have lots of care
L ove and help but not to scare
S top it right now.

Emily Norman (9)
Cherry Tree Primary School, Lymm

Litter

L et's go and put our rubbish in the bin
I f you litter our world you will commit a sin
T ry to pick up litter every day
T houghtfulness gives somewhere for children to play
E veryone must play their part
R ecognise the problem, don't break my heart.

Ellie Rimmer (9)
Cherry Tree Primary School, Lymm

Litter

Litter, litter, don't throw it on the floor
It makes our country dirty, we don't want anymore
A message to all people, keep the world clean
Our environment should remain green
Eat your food then find a bin
Let's not let the litter louts win!

Vicky Hewett (8)
Cherry Tree Primary School, Lymm

Let's Stop Litter

L et's stop litter
I t is so bitter
T ell your friends
T he world needs to mend
E veryone the litter has to stop!
R eally our world is not top.

Abbie Eleanor Blythe (9)
Cherry Tree Primary School, Lymm

Save The Planet!

We all can do that little bit more,
By turning off taps,
Reducing the climate change,
Reusing things that you find out and about,
Recycling paper, boxes and bottles,
Stop cutting down trees,
Pick up that little bit of litter
And put it in the bin!

Chloe Amanda Harrison (11)
Great Corby School, Carlisle

Green Poem

When you put things in the trash,
Stop and think, don't go too fast.
Because plastic, paper, cardboard and tins,
Can all be put in recycling bins.
Don't go in your cars, because it causes pollution,
Go on your bikes, that's the solution.
Cutting down forests, loses animals' homes,
And all you'll see of them is a pile of bones.
During the day it's nice and bright,
So save electricity, turn off the light.
Get involved and get keen
Come on everybody, go green!

Heather Lomax (11)
Great Corby School, Carlisle

Global Warming

Get out of your cars
And get out of that bus
Start walking and don't make a fuss.
Turn down your heating,
Switch off that light,
Make sure your TV is off at night.
If you cut down the forest where the animals roam,
You're destroying the place they call home.
Listen to me,
I'm telling it straight,
Change your ways, before it's too late.

Eden Bevington (10)
Great Corby School, Carlisle

Recycling

I love our planet, it is kind to me
So please stop littering
Recycle, it's better to save our
Tigers and snow leopards too.
Stop climate change.

I love our planet, so let's keep it green.

Stop war.
Stop disease.
Stop racism and poverty.
So we can all enjoy the world together.

Annie Smith (7)
Great Corby School, Carlisle

Go Green!

Don't throw your litter on the floor,
Reduce pollution and prevent climate change.

Rainforests are being cut down,
Animals are being made extinct.
The world is getting warmer.
We need to save the world now.
So go green!

Jamie Harrison (8)
Great Corby School, Carlisle

The War Of The Litterbug

The streets are full of rubbish.
The parks have dog mess in them.
Let's have more bins in our parks and streets,
So we can beat the litterbug creeps.
They treat this world like a great big dump,
Let's bin it to win it,
The war of the litterbug.

Evan Jones (9)
Great Corby School, Carlisle

Go Green

Put litter in the recycling bin
The world is getting hotter
We need some help now
Animals are becoming extinct
Rainforests are getting cut down
So go green!

Ewan Frith (8)
Great Corby School, Carlisle

Show Me

Show me a world without poverty
Show me a world without war
Show me a world without pollution
Show me a world without disease
Who can show me? Everyone can,
By doing a little bit to make a big difference.

Chloé Kennon (10)
Great Corby School, Carlisle

Recycling Is Good

Litter, litter, on the ground.
What a sight I have found.
Coke cans and lollipop sticks.
Oh dear, what a terrible shame this is.
Litter, litter, what a sin.
It should be in the bin.

Lowri Morris Williams (7)
Great Corby School, Carlisle

Litter!

Litter, rubbish, all this clutter
All this makes me stop and mutter.
Why do people pollute like this?
Why not recycle? What's to miss?

Samuel John Turnbull (7)
Great Corby School, Carlisle

Save Earth

S uffering nature is all around
A sking what to do when the ozone layer has gone
V acations polluting air and sea
E arth is suffering, help us now!

E xclude unnecessary electricity
A dvance to 2050 and cut the energy
R ecycle, reduce, reuse
T rains polluting the air
H abitats dying out.

Joe Black (11)
Havannah Primary School, Buglawton

Stop! Change! Change!

S is for saving the planet from climate change
T is for temperate to save the temperate climate
O is for ozone layer to save the ozone layer
P is for polar to help save the ice.

C is for cars causing pollution
L is for losing ozone layer
I is for igloos that are slowly melting
M is for muppets that are driving gas guzzling cars
A is for aeroplanes polluting our skies
T is for trains that take drivers off the road
E is for environment - a clean one we want.

C is for changing the way we live
H is for help to help us stop climate change
A is for arid, the cold days might go
N is for nations to combine us together
G is for gateway to a better world
E is for eco - please be eco-friendly.

Daniel Craddock (10)
Havannah Primary School, Buglawton

Save Earth Now!

S aving the planet
A lot of damage
V ital importance
E verlasting Earth

E co-friendly
A nimals' homes being destroyed
R eally bad gases
T ake action
H umans who never listen

N early destroyed Earth
O ver using energy
W ater levels going up.

Save Earth now!

George Aldington (10)
Havannah Primary School, Buglawton

Pity The Planet

P lanet Earth
I ce caps are melting
T ake care of the environment
Y ou are the only ones who can help

T he poor polar bears
H elp the planet
E arth has feelings too!

P ollution
L ove the world
A tmosphere is being polluted
N orth Pole won't be there for long
E arth needs our help
T he future of the planet depends on you . . .

George Murphy (10)
Havannah Primary School, Buglawton

Climate Change

C is for CO_2 emissions
L is for loss of animals
I is for irresponsible people
M is for making changes
A is for always recycle
T is for time running out
E is for everyone can help.

C is for causing pollution
H is for homeless people
A is for animals becoming extinct
N is for non-stop wasting
G is for getting people to learn about the environment
E is for environment - we all should care.

Vicky Harding (10)
Havannah Primary School, Buglawton

Save Our Earth

S ea levels are rising
A nimals are becoming endangered
V ital sources of energy are being lost
E veryone can help

O nly use your car when you really need to
U se less electricity
R educe, reuse, recycle

E arth is changing every day
A nd all the ice is melting
R espect the environment
T he future of our planet depends on you
H elp Earth now.

Katie Smith (10)
Havannah Primary School, Buglawton

The Suffering World

A suffering world under a breaking atmosphere,
Destroying everything we own and again,
Each day, ice caps melt quite a bit more,
Making this world a living hell.

This world is covered in litter,
Polluting the air and causing illness,
Flood barriers are starting to give way,
Wars aren't things of the past.

Carbon dioxide is growing fast,
Diseases are spreading worldwide,
Water and food is becoming unsafe,
The world is changing day by day.

Jacob Lea (11)
Havannah Primary School, Buglawton

Tigers

These fascinating creatures are becoming extinct
They're black and white and orange
They know how to fight.

These animals are very rare
That's why they can hardly be found anywhere.

People in the future may never see
How beautiful these creatures can actually be.
They start off as cubs
Then grow.

Brothers and sisters follow in tow . . .

Poachers kill for their coats of fur
Because they're selfish and cannot bear for tigers to be seen.

Help bring tigers out of extinction, to help others see how beautiful
These creatures can actually be.

Joshua Wild (9)
Hursthead Junior School, Cheadle Hulme

Tigers' Wildlife

Tigers pounce, soaring, shooting,
Leaping elegantly, landing gracefully.
Colourful stripes, soothing fur.

Tiger, tiger, burning bright.
William Blake wrote about you
So powerful you're King of the Jungle.

Fast as wind,
Fast as lightning,
Storming, strolling, pouncing with joy.

Camouflage but outstanding,
Gobsmacked when we see you
All the tigers want to play.

Pads pounce,
Mysteriously peeping,
Curiously peering,
Slowly stepping.

Staring, avoiding
The animals ahead
Growling while swaying.

Frightened when they come to you
With daggers, ready to hate.
If you are one be warned,
Beware! The tigers are becoming extinct.

Beth Russell (9)
Hursthead Junior School, Cheadle Hulme

The Bengal Tiger

I am one of the few tigers here.
I saw an animal, an animal I could eat.
I leapt for it but it wasn't that near.
I have no friends now, they have all died.

My colours are bright.
I look calm but angry and upset on the inside.
When I pounce my enemy has a fright.
When I'm not hungry, I lazily strut around.

I see tree trunks and leaves on the dusty floor.
Smaller insects stare at me wondering if I'll pounce.
Tree cutters come but don't think we are poor.
There are hardly any animals now to eat,
They have been killed too.

I am hot and confused.
Where have the trees gone?
What more am I going to lose?
What are these animals who walk on their hind legs?

Our home is disappearing,
Our friends are disappearing too.
Me and the remaining tigers will start searching,
Where will we go?

Siân Walsh (9)
Hursthead Junior School, Cheadle Hulme

Tigers

Only a few tigers are left in the world
In about five years they will be all gone
They are sleek and brave and powerful
We don't want there to be none.

The distant crashing of a waterfall
The dusty feel of the hot baked Earth
The fresh smell of the jungle
The birds singing their dawn chorus.

The tigers in the world are endangered
Running, panting and fighting to keep safe
We have got to help these sad creatures
They all deserve to live.

The beautiful smell of water
On top of the emerald leaves
Once again help these survivors
Or they will die, so please . . .

The orange and black on their soft fur
They leap and pounce on their prey
The poachers in the distance
Killing them every day.

Rachel Lewis (9)
Hursthead Junior School, Cheadle Hulme

Without A Home

As I fall asleep on my cold and soggy bed,
My head is whirling with all of the distant memories,
In my mind my mum is standing there beaming at me,
Her arms are wide open and I run towards her,
Then I wake suddenly with a blanket of snow on me,
Tears are streaming down my face, another awful winter's day.

I'm in the London underground, slouching in a corner,
My money pot is empty and my lips are desert dry
People walk right past me as if I am not there.
Still I can hear my mother's words, 'Don't worry, I will find you again some day.'

All I want is a family and a house to live in,
Food and drink would be the greatest things.
I want to be treated equally, and I need to be safe
Why did this happen to me?
Here I am then, deflated and crestfallen,
Back in the stone-cold park.
I feel really weak and weary
I drift off silently
To the place where my mother awaits me.

Andrew Hargreaves (10)
Hursthead Junior School, Cheadle Hulme

Help Save The Bengal Tigers

She is the fiercest animal on Earth.
Sleek and strong and fast.
She hunts for her prey.
Powerfully watching for food for her cubs.
She is there, camouflaged in action.
Other Bengal tigers have been killed,
For medicines and clothing, food.
Her habitat is almost destroyed for wood and paper.
She lives in a small forest with five cubs.
Two girls, three boys.
The others have been killed.
She is trying to help save her cubs,
And we are trying to save all of the Bengal tigers.
She is a mum.
The dad died with the cubs.
She and her cubs will need help, and they will need it, and fast!

Please, please can you help!
We need help, and they need help.
Join us to save the Bengal tigers!

Annabel Scriven (9)
Hursthead Junior School, Cheadle Hulme

A Tree's Life

I rustle and whisper,
I'm old but skyscraping
I give oxygen and food,
I'm all bumpy and rigid,
I give wood for people to use.

People climb me and
In the summer I shade people,
Eventually I get cut down.

Daisy Miles (7)
Hursthead Junior School, Cheadle Hulme

The Tree Poem

Magnolia
Whitey pink soft carpet, gentle
Sound, smooth trees help people to breathe
They help animals, autumn, yellow, brown
Red, golden crunchy noise, crispy
Climbing tree,
Small, thick,
Rough, bumpy,
Rings tell the
Age, beautiful
Blossom, bright,
It looks like
A y shape,
Wind, floating
Down slowly
Side to side
To make a
Carpet of them
Collecting, recycling.

Max Reed (7)
Hursthead Junior School, Cheadle Hulme

The World Is Wonderful

Flowers blooming by a turquoise stream
Wild bunnies hoping across the lawn.
This is how our world should be.

Where the rabbits' burrows used to be now a mound
Of rusty cans, burst bin bags, smashed glass bottles,
Are all you can see.

Why do people spoil our world?
If everybody did something to help the world,
It would look a nicer place!

Emilia Mastrolonardo (8)
Hursthead Junior School, Cheadle Hulme

Tree Poem

Tall oak tree with
Birds singing, rough, bumpy bark.
Squirrels scurrying with sharp claws
Collecting cold acorns on the bumpy
Branches. New fresh green leaves growing
Calmly, carefully and slowly.
Green
New
Fresh
Leaves
Falling
Off the
Trees onto
The
Ground.
Green
Soft leaves
Furry.

Molly Whelan (7)
Hursthead Junior School, Cheadle Hulme

Tigers

Black and orange stripes of beauty,
Shimmering in the midday sun.
The majestic tiger crawls silently across the overgrown grass.
Leaping carelessly in the breeze he crosses the beautiful stream.
His emerald eyes glimmer in the sun, enjoying freedom, that's what he does.
He feels the wind brush against his soft, gentle fur.
Hearing the lovely birds singing their song in the jungle sky.
Growling angrily at poachers, scaring them off with his ferocious roar.
His razor-sharp teeth, catching his prey.
This tiger is proud to be a tiger.

Edward McCue (9)
Hursthead Junior School, Cheadle Hulme

Do Not Destroy Tigers!

Tigers are great they really are,
Tigers will hunt for something to eat if it's close or far.
Why should we kill these wonderful animals?
They could be gone forever.
What wonderful smells tigers must have,
The smell of all the plants in the forest,
The smell of the jungle's fresh air.
What wonderful sight tigers must have,
Looking at animals, trees and plants.
With their stripes they look so brave,
So do not take these animals away.
Do not destroy these tigers' habitat,
The wonderful jungle where tigers live,
Do not destroy it or they'll have no place to live.
So if you're someone killing them,
Please don't because we might never see them again.
Oh so wonderful tigers they are,
Please do not destroy them.

Jamie Moffat (9)
Hursthead Junior School, Cheadle Hulme

The Lonely Girl

Lonely, upsetting tears running fast down her cheeks.
Watching children marching around the park.
Plods in fields seeing animals being fed.
Waits at bus stop ready for bus to pick her up.
Dirt in her hair, cold, suffering.
Reading old newspapers from rubbish bins.
Seeing family through the window, laughing together.
Dreams of a cosy bed, heating on.
Sitting at the dining table laughing with her family.
Eating a roast diner.
Pictures on the wall and cuddling up on the sofa, watching a movie.

Izzie Slater (10)
Hursthead Junior School, Cheadle Hulme

What I Imagine

I am homeless,
I am homeless,
I spend my days under an old bus shelter,
Thinking of a meal,
Thinking of a home,
A home with a fire to keep warm,
A home with clean water to wash and drink,
That's what I imagine.

I imagine a family,
A family who give me company,
A family who give me love,
That's what I imagine.

I don't imagine an old bus shelter,
I don't imagine a scruffy blanket,
I don't imagine a littered city,
I don't have to,
That's already here.

Shay Ward (10)
Hursthead Junior School, Cheadle Hulme

Tiger, Tiger Burning Bright

Swiftly, silently through the night,
This great big cat puts up quite a fight.
Big black stripes tell you beware.
Hunting deer, crouched down low,
Prowling round and round.
Run straight after it, down it's dead.
Yum-yum tucking into tea.
Seconds later it's all gone.
Now it's time for bed.
Fall asleep, full and tired,
Till dawn comes again.

Charlotte Whelan (9)
Hursthead Junior School, Cheadle Hulme

Homeless

The destitute old man wandered aimlessly down the old musty street of dilapidated houses banished of life, thinking longingly of how it used to be his home. Feeling so unlucky and lonely, why did it have to be him who lost his house and family, and personal belongings?

Every endless day was spent scrutinising all the dusty pavements for any scraps of food, every stone-cold chip or squashed grape. Yearning for the food his mother used to cook. He rummaged in all of the bins for unwanted food, anything edible would do. Meandering, dreamily along, looking enviously at the warm food through the house windows.

Every perishing night spent huddled up on a park bench, his trustworthy greyhound by his side with only each other for company and comfort. Lay there as the wind billowed around them, both snuggled under the same singed rug. Rain drenched them but they had no other place to go, all he wished for was a warm home with a loving family.

Rebecca Bardsley (10)
Hursthead Junior School, Cheadle Hulme

Tiger, Tiger Burning Bright

Tiger, tiger amber eyes,
With your glow, light the night,
Tiger, tiger run your distance,
Tiger, tiger elegant stance, with puffy whiskers.
The bark of the black tree hide behind,
The poachers are coming, you beware,
They might kill you like a hare.
Rest your head on the dark, black rock,
Feel the soft, light green moss,
And go to sleep, forget your loss,
Go to eat in your little hut,
Rest your head once again, after you have had your meal,
And be prepared, they might come again,
And live your life within your den.

Matthew Ashpole (9)
Hursthead Junior School, Cheadle Hulme

No One Cares

One more woman lying on the austere streets of London,
Sleeping in a small gap that is now her den.
Clothes in bags and dressed in rags, and hair in straggly strands.
Eating from small and almost empty cans.
A once rich family,
A husband that was manly,
But no one really cared.

Dreaming of warmth and a bed,
In which she can rest her head.
Food enough to last the year,
Where family are always near,
Dreaming of a once rich family,
Of a husband that was manly,
But knowing no one really cares.

Jessany Marsden (10)
Hursthead Junior School, Cheadle Hulme

Wandering The Streets Of London

He wanders the streets of London looking for shelter,
A bus stop, a train station, anything will do,
How he dreams of a small cottage like he used to have,
He wanders feeling sorrowful and dejected.

He is like an abandoned dog with no one to care for him.
His clothes in rags and his stomach empty.
Every night he begs for money but is not successful,
He is desperate for a friend.

He carries his home two carrier bags,
Every evening he reminds himself of the good times past.
When he had a family and the warm cottage he dreams about,
He is longing for a home.

Anna Russell (10)
Hursthead Junior School, Cheadle Hulme

I See . . . I See . . .

Every day I see a lonely, poor, old woman
Walking the cobbly streets of London.
She is carrying her home in bags.
I see her try to give the charity shops some of her clothes,
But they refuse to take the bags of dirty, scruffy, tatty clothes.
I see her roaming through the bins, desperately.
I can see she dreams of a mattress with a pillow and a blanket.
Her clothes are in rags,
They are torn and worn out.
She has greasy, grey, dirty hair.
Under her eyes are ebony, black bags.
Her unfulfilled eyes are saying, please talk to me.

Kirsten Williams-Lee (10)
Hursthead Junior School, Cheadle Hulme

The World Should Be Wonderful

The world should be wonderful all around.
The lovely glow of the moon and the sun,
Wildlife, animals, people and nature growing all the time,
Gardens and seasons different all around,
Butterflies and birds of every colour.
Let's recycle everyone.
Glass, cardboard, paper and tins.
Mountains stand high above us.
So if you want to keep this world like this,
Don't throw litter on the floor.
Keep tidy and much more.
So save the world!

Lauryn Shaw (8)
Hursthead Junior School, Cheadle Hulme

The Wonderful World!

The world is a wonderful place to be
With animals, butterflies, flowers and trees.
With beautiful countryside and mountains too,
We'll all look after it, me and you.
Let's recycle every day,
Cardboard, paper, bottles and tins,
Clothing, shoes, plastic and wood.
Let's all do the world some good!
Never litter, keep the world clean, just put your rubbish in the bin!
The moon and the sun just shine so bright,
They look so pretty in the bright blue sky.
So the world is nice to live in now!

Ella Morton (8)
Hursthead Junior School, Cheadle Hulme

The Lonely Girl

Under the arches is where she sleeps,
With the rats and stray dogs,
All she has to keep warm is an old blanket
Roaming the streets, begging for money.

Unappreciated and depressed, is how she feels,
Damp and dirty with no clean clothes,
Fighting for survival as she tries to get to sleep,
Rummaging through the bins, looking for something to eat.

Carrying her possessions in worn-out carrier bags,
Dreaming of a better life as she looks up at the magnified moon,
Fortune has dealt its cards and left her out.

Georgia Dee-Upton (10)
Hursthead Junior School, Cheadle Hulme

Mystery Man

I can see the desperate old man begging for money
Alongside the pavement, everyone ignoring the fact
That he's starving and homeless.
A solitary guy, lonely for no comfort and hungry,
No crumbs of food, shuffling sluggishly down the misty road,
Thinking of nothing but a home and family.

He wishes for happiness and friendliness, but he'll hardly get it,
His dream is to live in a home full of fresh food, cosy warm bed and family.
He is completely spiritless and hostile,
Wearing but only fragments of cloth all torn and ripped with no shoes.

Stephen Harwood (10)
Hursthead Junior School, Cheadle Hulme

Look At The World

Look at the world around you
The trees and the bees

The elephants and crocodiles
The plants and the sea

But all this lovely wonder
It really makes me ponder

Why they don't recycle?
It's absolutely vital

The Earth will soon cloud over
All the birds will die
And all the yummy fruit so we won't have a pie

But if we do our little bit, our little bit each day
The birds will soon come back and the cloud will move away

So now that I've told you, please do what I've said
Recycle, recycle until you are dead!

Jessica Pullan (10)
Kirkoswald CE Primary School, Kirkowsald

Save The Bees

I wonder what the world would be,
Without a single wasp or bee,
Not a single leaf upon each tree,
What a miserable planet it would be.

Do you know what you can do,
To save the animals in the zoo?
Well you could plant a tree or two,
Or recycle things with no further use to you.

In the future we should see,
Another few million bright green trees,
Over one hundred wasps and bees,
And as for the fish in the sea,
I can almost guarantee,
Many more of them you will see,
Providing you go eco.

Victoria Ironmonger (10)
Kirkoswald CE Primary School, Kirkowsald

Blue And Green

The things that you can do with blue . . .
I don't know how about you?

What about the sky? What about the sea?
What about the blue birds in the tree?

The things that you can do with green . . .?
I don't know, wait and see. The grass, the trees . . .
What about the green wheelie bins?

As you see the world is full of blue and green.
Think about trees and sky - what a beautiful scene.

Jade Bibby (10)
Kirkoswald CE Primary School, Kirkowsald

Beasts And Birds

Dogs, cats, dogs, cats
Mice, rats, mice, rats
All the things that live on Earth
As well as the kangaroos in Perth
Need the love and TLC
That we don't give to all we see.
So come on, get started now
To save all things but you'll say, 'How?'
This is how you can help
To save all things that roar and yelp:

Reduce, reuse, recycle
Or adopt an animal today
Like a horse that nibbles on the hay.
Everything needs your help, so start, don't hesitate,
If you want to see a badger at your gate.

Joe Dodd (9)
Kirkoswald CE Primary School, Kirkowsald

Help The Earth

The Earth is in trouble,
If we don't help it will be double,
The trees are going one by one,
If we keep doing this there will be none.

Life is in threat,
Life will be wet,
You will bet,
We own the world's debt.

The world feels too,
Let's make sure we treat it like jewels.

Poetry machine
You will always be green!

Lewis Wyatt-Taylor (9)
Kirkoswald CE Primary School, Kirkowsald

Go Green, Recycle

G o green
O range? Let's pass

G reat things may change
R ecycling will stop this
E nergy will stop
E ven though you have a home . . .
N ot everyone does

R educe your carbon footprint
E veryone . . .
C ome on!
Y ou could help save the world!
C ould there actually be life on Mars?
L et's recycle and see!
E xtinction? Let's pass as well!

Chloe Boston (10)
Kirkoswald CE Primary School, Kirkowsald

Pollution

P lease save planet Earth and recycle.
O nly you can stop pollution
L itter's such a killer! Please help us clean up this
L itter.
U nderground there's so much rubbish, don't know how moles survive
T o help the trees, recycle paper.
I ncredible amounts of waste on Earth.
O range trees will soon be gone.
N ow is the time to act.

Joseph Wilcock (10)
Kirkoswald CE Primary School, Kirkowsald

Litter - Recycle Please!

Rubbish, litter all around
Plastic bottles to be found
Do you think it's a good idea
For all the waste to be so near?
Cans and pans and metal things
Should not be put in your bins
Listen, there is another way
To do some good and save the day.
A little thought is all it takes to change the state we're in
It means you just need to use the recycle bin.

Matthew Dalton (8)
Kirkoswald CE Primary School, Kirkowsald

Going Green Poem

Do not take your car to school, because it may look like fun
But you might be dumb
Just walk up and that's the solution!

If you waste any food
You are not a cool dude.

Always remember to turn off the tap
And I'll let you borrow my favourite map.
Don't waste water!

James Hitch (7)
Kirkoswald CE Primary School, Kirkowsald

Recycle

Recycle, recycle, there is a cycle.
The cycle of recycling.

Where you recycle a tyre and it
Magically turns to gold.

Recycle, recycle that is a magic cycle.
The cycle of recycling.

Which makes the world a better place!

Iona Frost (10)
Kirkoswald CE Primary School, Kirkowsald

Rubbish

Rubbish, rubbish don't drop it down,
Use a recycle bin to help all around.
Rubbish, rubbish does it stink?
Not if you stop and think.
Wash your bottles, wash your cans,
Help make this a greener land.
Rubbish, rubbish, away, don't throw,
Let's all recycle, go! Go! Go!

Harriet Park (8)
Kirkoswald CE Primary School, Kirkowsald

Go Green

Green, green my favourite colour
Green, green the colour of trees
Green, green the colour of the grass
But what about recycling?
If you don't recycle, think about the world
Think about animals
The polluted air . . .
So go green!

Olivia Temple-Cox (10)
Kirkoswald CE Primary School, Kirkowsald

The Green Machine

Recycling is easy . . .
Recycling is cool,
We are the energy savers,
At Leamington School.

Let's start with the bins,
Green, purple and blue,
We love to recycle,
And you can too.

Recycling is easy . . .
Recycling is cool,
We are the energy savers,
At Leamington School.

Turn off the tap
Put out the light
Pick up litter
And put it to right.

Chloe Shelbourne & Sophie Galbraith (10)
Leamington Primary School, Liverpool

Look At The World

Look at the world,
Is it beautiful?
No it's not
It's so pitiful.

Look at the world,
Lots of pollution.
Yes there is,
We need an evolution.

Look at the world
People destroying.
We should stop them
Because they're annoying.

Look at the world
Look at the range of people
Destroying the planet.
We need a change.

Look at the world
What can we do
To make it a better place
For me and for you?

Jonathan Hughes (10)
Legh Vale Primary School, Haydock

Litter

Litter, litter everywhere
Why do some of us never care
For anything that we show?
Listen to me and you will know
Plants need water to help them grow
Not dirty water, clean and fresh from the sky
And if they don't, they really will die.

Lauren Jade McLoughlin (10)
Legh Vale Primary School, Haydock

Pollution Poem

Don't use vehicles,
They will pollute the air,
And if you do,
Fumes will be here and there.

Walk instead of drive,
It will make you better,
For if you do,
You will make the world bitter.

Don't pollute the atmosphere,
You will ruin the weather,
If you do pollute,
People will reach the end of their tether.

Please don't pollute,
People will be sad,
But if you do,
You will be very bad.

Joshua Flanagan (10)
Legh Vale Primary School, Haydock

Care For The Environment

Do you care about the environment?
If you do you wouldn't dare to drop litter.
You should find a bin and put your litter in.
Recycle, reduce and reuse whenever you can,
And do your bit to help.
Switch the TV off when you leave the room,
And switch the light off.
Walk whenever you can and save lots of energy.
Look what we have done to our world,
Animals are dying, and others are crying.
So save our planet if you care!

Lucy Hughes (10)
Legh Vale Primary School, Haydock

Save Our Earth

Water pollution
Air pollution
Global warming means
A wrong solution.

All of the factories
Are creating fumes and smoke
And if we're not careful
We could choke.

Why don't people turn lights off?
Why do factories pollute the air?
Why do people do it?
It's not fair!

Emma Simpson (10)
Legh Vale Primary School, Haydock

Help Our World

H elp the world
E veryone has to recycle
L iving in this world is a disgrace
P eople are destroying our world.

O ur planet is being polluted
U se recycle bags
R euse what you can

W ould you like to save our world?
O ur world is a disgrace
R emember to look after our planet
L et's clean up
D o it now!

Alice Forber (7)
Legh Vale Primary School, Haydock

Litter Everywhere

Litter, litter everywhere
Even in the park that me and you share.
Litter, litter everywhere
Even in the public places that me and you share.
Litter, litter everywhere
Why do some people not care?
Litter, litter everywhere
That shows how eco-friendly you are.
Litter, litter everywhere
Killing things that live on Earth.
Litter, litter everywhere
Litter is making our world untidy.

Mollie O'Hara (10)
Legh Vale Primary School, Haydock

Don't Forget To Recycle

Can crunching
Bottle bashing
Paper punching
Plastic plunging
Sauce bottle screwing
Carton crumbling
Soda bottle splitting
Don't ruin our world
Recycle
Make the world a better place
For the whole entire human race
Are you going to recycle?

Rebecca Cliffe (10)
Legh Vale Primary School, Haydock

Save the Animals

I feel sorry for the animals
Because they are becoming extinct.

Would you rather wear a tiger,
Or see one in the wild?

Would you rather see a shark in the sea,
Or eat it for your tea?

Would you rather have a gorilla hand ashtray,
Or see them play?

It's up to you!

Lewis Grimshaw (7)
Legh Vale Primary School, Haydock

Things Are Dying

Think about our atmosphere
It is all dying from pollution
Just take care of it
Because we are
All becoming sad
Think about our planet
It could disappear
Try and make the world a better place
Trees are dying, animals are dying
Just think about it.

Eleanor Maloney-Ward (7)
Legh Vale Primary School, Haydock

Eco-Kids

Don't drop litter at any time
Or the world will be filled with grime.
If you do you will get a fine,
So don't drop litter at any time.
The fish are dying and we are crying,
Because of the horrible litter on the floor.
When you can put it in the bin
It is a crime and if you get caught,
You will get fined,
Don't drop litter at any time.

Katie Gray (11)
Legh Vale Primary School, Haydock

Animals

Saving animals is a good thing to do
Little animals are dying and some have already
I really care about them all
Help every animal in the universe
And I am pretty sure animals want to live too
Try very hard to help animals like tigers and gorillas
Animals want to live too
I love animals and I hope you do too
Loving animals is a good thing!

Millie McDonagh (7)
Legh Vale Primary School, Haydock

Save Our World!

Fish are dying,
Animals are crying,
Mammals are going extinct,
Take some time to think,
Help to stop pollution,
It's the only solution,
Don't be bitter,
Don't drop litter,
Save our world!

Heath Taylor (10)
Legh Vale Primary School, Haydock

Save The Animals

Save the panda
Save the chimp
Save the hippo
Save the tiger
Because all the children in the future
Would like to see them
Save the fish
Save the environment
Help stop pollution in the world.

Matthew Crosby (10)
Legh Vale Primary School, Haydock

Recycling

R ecycling is important
E verything must be recycled
C lothes can be recycled
Y ou must keep the world clean
C arrier bags must be recycled
L itter can be picked up and recycled
I f you recycle you can save the world
N ever litter!
G ive the world a better chance!

Joe White (8)
Legh Vale Primary School, Haydock

Stop Wasting, Start Recycling

Did you know,
Around our world is the ozone layer,
And it is disappearing?

Did you know that we are polluting by using cars?
It's not too late, can you help?
Start switching off lights, because it is saving energy
And stop the pollution.
Now you're helping.

Jordan Shaw (9)
Legh Vale Primary School, Haydock

Try To Be Eco

Try to be eco even Chico is eco.
These are some things that are happening.
Animals dying, animals crying,
Too much buying.
The bought things should be recycled.
If we walk, if we ride, even if you slide,
It doesn't matter what you do, but try not to go in cars.
If we do all these things, then you will feel like a queen or a king.

Daniel Cummings (10)
Legh Vale Primary School, Haydock

Putting Litter In The Bin

Have a clean world
So don't drop litter on the floor.
Put it in the bin
Then the world will be happy.
Put plastic bottles and cans in the recycle bin
Then we will be happy!
Keep the forest clean
So the animals will be happy.

Ben O'Toole (7)
Legh Vale Primary School, Haydock

Global Warming

The animals are dying, people are crying,
The Earth is going to stop turning.
Towns are flooding, trees are crumbling,
Pollution is pouring,
But people are ignoring,
And soon the Earth will be dead.

Matthew Johnston (11)
Legh Vale Primary School, Haydock

Save The Environment!

Save the environment
Things are dying
Save the environment
Litter on the ground
Save the environment
Pollution in the air
Save the environment
We have to care!

Matthew Marsden (11)
Legh Vale Primary School, Haydock

Help Save The World

The Earth, the Earth is where we all share life
So don't drop litter, it's not right,
We all should work together to keep it clean
Also recycle so it will make life better indeed.
Please don't drop litter on the floor,
It would be better if you did not at all.
Pollution, pollution is going in the air,
So try to stop it because it can be dangerous.

Sam Portwood (10)
Legh Vale Primary School, Haydock

Eco Kid

The eco kid saves trees,
Come and help us, please.
The eco kid recycles,
He always rides his bicycle.
The eco kid stops animals dying,
Please stop them crying.

Daniel James Harper (10)
Legh Vale Primary School, Haydock

River, River

River, river in the world
Come to me to see the world.
River, river in the sea
Let me paddle while you see.
River, river by the tree
You float and shoot, so let me see.
River, river in the world
We love you and that is so.

Lauren Henshaw (10)
Legh Vale Primary School, Haydock

Heal The world

Heal the world, right this minute
Or it will backfire to the limit.
When the time is right
The world will shine ever so bright.
Let's turn green,
Don't be mean.
Let's turn fast
And the world will be class.

Callum Thomas Proctor (10)
Legh Vale Primary School, Haydock

Don't Be A Litterbug

Litter, litter everywhere
We can change it if you care,
Throw your litter it looks a disgrace,
Make our planet a better place.
Recycle, recycle how much you can like metal,
And bottles you certainly can!

Rebecca Brown (10)
Legh Vale Primary School, Haydock

Animals

A nimals are going
N o more tigers to be seen
I nsects are dying
M onkeys are going
A frica will lose its life
L ovely sunsets will disappear
S ee the beautiful animals!

Luke Miles (7)
Legh Vale Primary School, Haydock

Recycle, Don't Kill The Earth

R ecycle don't litter
E nvironment keep clean
C ans recycle
Y ou're killing the world
C ardboard recycle
L itter is wrong
E arth is being killed because you're littering.

Jordan Plant
Legh Vale Primary School, Haydock

Save The Planet

Fish are dying,
Animals are crying,
Mammals are becoming extinct,
Take time to think,
Stop the pollution,
It's the only solution,
The Earth needs your help.

Thomas Grimshaw (10)
Legh Vale Primary School, Haydock

Think!

Think! The animals are going to be extinct,
We need your help quick,
They're dying and crying,
Reduce, recycle, reuse,
Litter dropping everywhere, do your bit,
Don't just drop it anywhere!
It's our world, think!

Stephanie Clark (10)
Legh Vale Primary School, Haydock

How?

Animals are dying
People are crying
Trees are dying
Pollution is rising
The Earth is full of litter
And it smells bitter
Global warming is forming.

David Martindale (10)
Legh Vale Primary School, Haydock

Save Our Planet

Save the tiger,
Save the dolphin,
Save the mammals of the world.
Save the trees,
Save the world,
Save the animals because they are going extinct.
Save the world before it is too late.

Daniel Anders (10)
Legh Vale Primary School, Haydock

Rainforest

I'm the rainforest man
I'm like a dream to you
So don't tear me apart
Don't cut up my trees
And never throw things in my waterfall.
So make a better place
And fill the world with peaceful harmony.

Amy Craig (8)
Legh Vale Primary School, Haydock

Litter!

Litter dropping should
Be stopping,
Sort it out, put it out,
Plastic, paper, garden rot,
Look after this planet,
It's all we've got.

Keiran Thompson (10)
Legh Vale Primary School, Haydock

World

W e have to save the world
O ur future will end
R uining the streets
L ittle animals are getting killed
D on't drop litter.

James Simpson (7)
Legh Vale Primary School, Haydock

Recycle, Recycle, Recycle

Paper, plastic and glass too,
We can all make a difference, to help the world through,
Recycle these and save the world,
We can save the planet, to be free from our fear,
We can save our planet, and we can make it stay here!

Jade Barry (10)
Legh Vale Primary School, Haydock

The Waste

Recycle, recycle, it's like a life cycle,
Recycle a can, it could get turned into part of a van!
Reuse, reuse, or I'll blow a fuse!
Reuse a plastic bag or the world will begin to sag.
Reduce, reduce, like my aunt Goose.

Aarron Hill (10)
Legh Vale Primary School, Haydock

I Have A Solution For Pollution

P lease don't use the car, only if you need to
O zone layer is being destroyed because of you
L ovely countries like China are getting smoggy
L ots of people have to live where it's foggy
U se less energy, turn off the lights
T iny little things you do will give you a fright
I n your home you need to recycle
O r don't get a bus, get on your bicycle
N obody wants to live where it's foggy.

Abigail Lawrence (10)
Linacre Primary School, Bootle

Save The World

P ollution is horrible
O il is a waste
L itter on the floor
L ots of people drop litter
U nder clouds rats play around
T ime is gone
I n our world
O n day two let's pick up litter
N ow let's bin it!

Lewis McMurrie (10)
Linacre Primary School, Bootle

Litter

Please don't drop litter,
An eyesore to our landscape.
Messy, dirty streets.
Litter spoils the beach.
It is very heartbreaking,
Horrible to see.
If you have litter,
Don't throw it all around you,
Keep our planet clean!

Georgia Sumnall (8)
Marlfields Primary School, Congleton

Save The World

Leaves everywhere, pick them up.
Trees are being cut down fast.
Most things are dying out.
Recycle plastic bags.

Harrison Rhodes (9)
Milnrow Parish CE Primary School, Milnrow

Animal Captivity

Animal captivity is a cruel thing,
Birds cannot spread a wing,
Children like to laugh,
Animals can't run down a path.

If you keep them in cages,
Then you don't know the ages.
Come and set the animals free,
Into the wild and let them see.

Give them more meat,
And less heat.
Let them have a clean life,
Also a happy life.

Animals are part of the world,
So if you give them freedom.
We will be happy and so will you,
They will be more caring,
So set them free into the world!

Chloé Bingham & Amber Barnes (10)
Milnrow Parish CE Primary School, Milnrow

Tin Foil

I went to get an orange from the fruit bowl
I opened it and all it was, was tinfoil
So I opened the tin foil and it was just tin foil
So I went upstairs and said to Mum,
'Why is there tin foil in this orange?'
Mum said, 'Because it's for your brother's
Recycling day tomorrow.'
So I walked behind my brother and found people are
Recycling.

Emily Thwaites (8)
Milnrow Parish CE Primary School, Milnrow

Enclosed Elephant

My heart turned to stone,
When I saw the elephant all alone.
His eyes were closed,
As he was forced to pose.
His legs were pinned,
So I cried for him.
It was later that I learned by chance,
That he was made to dance.
So I hurried back to see,
The horrible owner not set him free.
But it was an awful thing I saw,
The elephant being poked by an old claw.
Weighed down by chains, so strong and thick,
While a poker poked him with a stick.
As the audience laughed with glee,
The elephant cried in misery,
But I didn't know what to do or say,
So I turned my back and crept away.

Emily Wong, Gemma Whatmough & Paige Ryan (10)
Milnrow Parish CE Primary School, Milnrow

Whales!

My pounding heart was moved to rage,
With whales getting trapped at a very young age,
From the sea, to the net,
Onto the land and out from the wet.
With a sad face and droopy eyes,
My face was shocked with a big surprise,
Stuffed in a pool with nothing to do,
Except eat and drink, got no friends to talk to
As the beast swam away,
As I had nothing else to say.
As I turned my back and walked away.

Nina Depasois (10) & Caitlin Morris (11)
Milnrow Parish CE Primary School, Milnrow

Animals' Extinction

Animals are dying,
We are really trying,
To help them survive,
Through their lives.

Hunters are bad,
They make me real mad.
They trap the little puny paws
With their steel jaws.

They kill them for their hair,
It isn't really fair,
It makes them really bare,
They don't really care.

Goodbye animals,
You're my real good friends,
I hope this bad thing ends,
I'll help until it mends.

James McDaid, Kieran Parry & Owen Thompson (10)
Milnrow Parish CE Primary School, Milnrow

Pollution

P lease recycle
O r reuse as
L ots of animals are dying and
L ots of people are dying
U nless we look after the world and recycle
T here will be too much litter to cope with
I t leads to global warming and
O zone pollution causes breathing and heart problems,
Overall a bad thing
N oise pollution can lead to hearing loss,
Sleep disturbance and stress. Not good at all.

Emily Figg (9)
Milnrow Parish CE Primary School, Milnrow

It's Good To Be Green

All this talk of being green
I asked my mum, 'What does it mean?'
Using less power, turning heating down
Recycling what we can to support our local town
Paper, cardboard, plastic, tins
We don't just put them into bins
Clothes can be passed on to people
Not as lucky as us
Refugees and poor people
Children just like me, except they live in poverty.
Mum says climate change will affect us all
Snow in June, Sun in October and
Increased annual rainfall.
I believe if we all do our bit
Turning lights off and recycling will keep our planet fit.
It's not that difficult to be a bit more green
The difficulty is, keeping everyone keen.

Nina Depasois (10)
Milnrow Parish CE Primary School, Milnrow

Making The World A Better Place

Litter goes in the bin,
Not in a tin,
Not on the floor,
Knock on the door.
Birds get strangled,
Dogs get mangled.
You'll be homeless,
Recycle,
Save the cycle.

Amy Reeves (10)
Milnrow Parish CE Primary School, Milnrow

Tortured Koala Bear

My throbbing heart was moved to rage,
When I saw that koala in its cage.
Its fur was dirty, its baby was dead,
Her mouth was dry, and her foot had bled.
It was later that I learned by chance,
The koala's owner made her sing,
Whilst hitting her with a piece of string.
And so I hurried back to see,
The wretched creature singing for me.
But it was an awful thing I saw,
As it had bruises and cuts on its paw,
Arms tied up and legs tied down,
The man stood next to her with a frown.
The crowd clapped and laughed with glee,
But all I wanted to do was set it free.
But I didn't know what to say or do,
So I turned my back and crept away!

Eva Whellans & James Scott (10)
Milnrow Parish CE Primary School, Milnrow

Pollution

Pollution is everywhere
Oil is very bad, it makes fish die
It can do horrible things wherever you go
It seems to me that everything is horrible
Use bins to put things in
The bins are for you to put things in
It is horrible and disgusting in the dustbins
On the way to the tip you can smell it
Now we can not smell anything.

Tom Whatmough (8)
Milnrow Parish CE Primary School, Milnrow

Tiger

My young heart was moved to rage,
When I saw the tiger inside the cage.
His fur was faded, his eyes were dim,
His teeth were blunt and I cried for him.
I only just learned by chance,
That the tiger's owner made him prance,
And so I hurried back to see,
The beautiful creature prancing free,
But it was an awful thing that I saw,
A broken beast with broken paws.
His freedom stopped by big steel bars,
No scenery, not anything but cars,
As the crowd clapped and laughed with glee,
As the beast roared for once to be free.
But I didn't know what to do or say,
So I turned my back and crept away.

Andrew Bedford (10)
Milnrow Parish CE Primary School, Milnrow

Ostrich, Oh Ostrich

How the small ostrich waits,
For the men to take away his fate,
His legs were cramped,
His feathers were damped.
He pecked, he pecked, at anyone near,
Because he was in so much fear.
So how I hurried back to see,
The ostrich gobbling his dirty tea.
How I saw the people laugh with glee,
Kicking around his dignity.
Ostrich, oh ostrich,
How will I revive of what I've seen,
But I do hope you survive.

Bradley Turner (11) & Owen Thompson (10)
Milnrow Parish CE Primary School, Milnrow

The King Of The Jungle

My young heart was moved to rage,
When I saw the King inside the cage,
His mane was filthy, his eyes were dim.
His tail was scruffy, and I cried for him.
It was later that I learned by law,
The lion's owner made him roar,
And so I rushed back to see,
The beautiful species roaring free.
But it was a horrid thing I saw,
A scabby beast with a broken paw,
Held down by locks so tough and thick,
While a man prodded him with a stick.
The crowd jumped and leapt with glee,
As the lion roared on in misery.
But I didn't know what to do or say,
So I turned my back and crept away.

Chloé Bingham & Laura Aspinall (10)
Milnrow Parish CE Primary School, Milnrow

Pollution

P lease recycle all you can
O pen your hearts for these poor animals that are beginning to die
L ook at your world, how it is crumbling up
L onely, trying to survive, please help to provide
U p and up the pollution comes
T he world is breaking up, it is like you don't care
I f your world just crumbles up and dies
O n and on the pollution grows
N ever throw litter around, because it can destroy the Earth.

Amy Aspinall (8)
Milnrow Parish CE Primary School, Milnrow

Parrot

My young heart turned to rage
When I saw the parrot in its cage.
His feathers were dirty, his eyes were dim
His beak was battered, I cried for him.
It was later I learned by chance
The parrot's owner made it dance.
And so I hurried back to see
The harmless parrot singing free.
It was an awful thing I saw
A broken bird on a lumbering claw.
Weighed down by ropes so thick
I was so upset it made me sick.
The crowd clapped and laughed with glee
As the parrot sung in misery.
But I didn't know what to do or say
So I turned my back and ran away.

Kyran Holt, Sam Pickering & John Figg (11)
Milnrow Parish CE Primary School, Milnrow

The Forest

Trees make up the woods
Mist drifting with the wind
Men getting closer
Chopping for firewood
Voices of the animals calling in the dark
Birds flying by
Owls call for night.

Nathan David Rigby (7)
Milnrow Parish CE Primary School, Milnrow

Dolphin

My young heart was moved to rage,
When I saw a dolphin in an underwater cage,
His tail was cut, his eyes were dim,
His nose was cut, slit and I cried for him.
It was later than I learned by chance,
His trainer made him shake and dance
And as I hurried back to see,
The poor creature trying to shake free.
But it was an awful thing I saw,
A broken creature with a broken jaw,
Weighed down by chains, so strong and thick,
While a man prodded him with a stick.
The crowd laughed and clapped with glee,
As the dolphin danced in misery.
But I didn't know what to do or say,
So I turned my back and walked away.

Thomas Fitzgerald, Kieran Parry (11) & James McDaid (10)
Milnrow Parish CE Primary School, Milnrow

Save Our Planet, Save Our World

L ots of people throw their litter
I n the rivers which makes us bitter
T errible things are happening to our fish
T his is our only wish
E co friendly is how we want to be
R euse your rubbish, that is the key.

Megan O'Brien & Jade Colderley (8)
Milnrow Parish CE Primary School, Milnrow

The Horse In Pain

My young heart sank
As I looked at the cage
I saw the horse and I filled with rage
The horse was in pain
As it started to rain
The crowd all laughed at the horse again
It was later that I learned by chance
The horse's owner made him dance
And so I went back to see
The horse was not free
A hoof broke off
And stopped giving it straw
It was an awful thing I saw
So I turned my back and crept away.

Stephanie Prowse, Chelsea Elton & Kaydyn McWilliams (10)
Milnrow Parish CE Primary School, Milnrow

Koala

I saw a koala, angry with rage,
Trying to gnaw out of its cage,
Its tail was off and its eyes were dim,
It had a hook in its limb.
It had a broken paw and it was on the floor
Trying to breathe once more.
I saw a muzzle over its mouth to keep it quiet
And I thought I could start a riot.
A man picked it up by the scruff of its neck,
With a stick with a powerful prick
No one around was in tears, they were just laughing,
And drinking beers.
But I didn't know what to do or say,
So I turned my back and ran away.

Harrison Thomas & Charlie Proctor (10)
Milnrow Parish CE Primary School, Milnrow

Dogs

My young heart was moved to rage,
When I saw a dog inside the cage,
His fur was dirty, his eyes were dim,
His mouth was cold, I cried for him.
It was later that I learned by chance
The dog's owner made him prance.
So I hurried back to see the poor creature prancing free,
But it was awful, I saw a broken beast on a lumbering paw,
Weighed down by chains, so strong and thick,
While a man jabbed him with a whip.
The crowd clapped and laughed with glee
As the dog pranced around unhappily.
I didn't know what to do or say
So I turned my back and ran away!

Natalie McCormick (10)
Milnrow Parish CE Primary School, Milnrow

Climate Change

C limate change is everywhere
L osing Earth is a disgrace
I t's so bad I am going to faint
M aking pollution is so bad
A nd pass this on by one by one
T he green machine is so good
E ating Earth has gone too far.

C locks ticking everywhere, how much time?
H orrible yet I do not know. Too fast
A eroplanes go
N eed Earth to live
G oing to get too big!
E verything is going to burst!

Matthew Raines (8)
Milnrow Parish CE Primary School, Milnrow

Litter

L itter stop
I t's not fair to put things in the sea
T he animals are dying
T he birds are dying because of the oil
E at the food, don't waste it
R ecycle the bottle.

Caitlinn Maskrey (8)
Milnrow Parish CE Primary School, Milnrow

Litter

L oads of people and animals suffer from waste, so recycle it
I n places like the rainforest, animals are dying because of us
T oo many people are throwing things on the floor or in the air
T oo many things are going wrong, we need to sort things out
E verything is going wrong what will happen?
R otten people throw stuff on the floor.

Ben Murphy (8)
Milnrow Parish CE Primary School, Milnrow

Litter

L itter, litter stop dumping
I t causes problems
T ry to recycle
T ry to save the world!
E at the food, don't waste it
R ather recycle than waste.

Andrew Carter (9)
Milnrow Parish CE Primary School, Milnrow

Cars Making Pollution

Please stop your oil from leaking.
You are making a mess of the world.
Come on we can buy a good gold and black bike.
Wherever you or your friends are going in a car.
You and your friends are polluting.

Blake Whitelaw (8)
Milnrow Parish CE Primary School, Milnrow

Cars

C ars should not be used a lot
A car should not be used a lot because you waste a lot of oil
R ecycle tyres when they go flat
S top using too much oil because it costs a lot.

Charlotte Wilson (8)
Milnrow Parish CE Primary School, Milnrow

Litter

Litter, litter, horrible litter
I hate litter because it is bad
People think it is funny,
But they should recycle.

Rebecca Jane Mainwaring (9)
Milnrow Parish CE Primary School, Milnrow

Animal

A lways look after frightened animals
N ever hunt or kill animals
I f you destroy animals' homes, they won't have a home
M ore animals are dying every day
A nimals need caring for and will die with no food
L eave the animals in peace, to be happy forever more.

Lauren Roxburgh & Sophie O'Toole (8)
Netherton Moss Primary School, Netherton

Litter

L itter is bad for the Earth
I mprove your world, don't litter
T idy up our world
T o keep our streets clean, use the recycling bins
E nvironment is good, so don't mess it up
R ecycle your waste.

Anna O'Brien (8) & Stephanie McAlister (9)
Netherton Moss Primary School, Netherton

Litter

L itter is bad for the world
I don't want it on the floor
T ry to get it in the bin
T ogether we can do it
E veryone can do their bit
R ecycle, recycle, recycle.

Owen Doyle (8)
Netherton Moss Primary School, Netherton

Care For Our World

Litter, litter, litter, disappear from sight,
If I see any more I will have a fright
Care for our world.

Megan Taylor (7)
Netherton Moss Primary School, Netherton

Landfill Or Recycling

We all live on planet Earth,
It's our responsibility.
Keep the litter out of the way.
Landfills are not where it should stay.
We all live on planet Earth.
It's our responsibility.
Recycle all that you can,
Don't stick it in the black bin van.

We all live on planet Earth,
It's our responsibility.
Landfill is not good.
It is not what should
Be filling up the Earth.
We all live on planet Earth,
It's our responsibility.
Reduce,
Reuse,
And always
Recycle!

Emily Hillard (10)
Our Lady's RC Primary School, Aspull

Reduce, Reuse, Recycle

Litter, litter
It makes me feel bitter
It's a lot of mess
That can cause awful stress
So get a tin
And put in the bin
Recycling makes you feel
Better.

Cans, cans
Use your hands
To put them in the bin
Recycling makes you feel
Better.

Recycling, recycling
Reduce, reduce
Reuse, reuse
They all make you feel better.

Zoe Gaskell (9)
Our Lady's RC Primary School, Aspull

I Gave You Good Things

I gave you acres of rainforest
Just to have it thrown back in my face.
I gave you adoring landscapes,
You gave me graffited streets.
I gave you oceans of fish,
You gave me fishing tankers.
I gave you huge streams and rivers,
You gave me covering landfills.
The world is not a happy place,
I will give you one last chance.
Change the world today.

Jamie King (10)
Our Lady's RC Primary School, Aspull

I Give You, You Give Me

I give you beautiful scenery,
You give me rubbish tips.
I give you fields of wheat,
You give me miles of desert.
I give you quiet lanes,
You give me choked motorways.
I give you lazy rivers,
You give me clogged rivers.
I give you beautiful land,
You give me a landfill site.
I give you beautiful animals,
You give me skins of animals.
I give you the rainforest,
You give me woods of trees.
I give you everything nice,
You give me a terrible sight.

Do your bit and recycle.

James Lowe (10)
Our Lady's RC Primary School, Aspull

Litter

Litter, litter it is a disgrace
Recycle as much as you can
If we all played a role in helping
The environment,
What a better place it would be.
So don't go in the car, go on a bike,
Or go for a morning walk.

Most people don't care, they dump it anywhere.
One can on the floor in front of your door,
Just flick it in the bottle bin.
So do care for your environment.

Alex Ainscough (10)
Our Lady's RC Primary School, Aspull

The Environment Needs Our Help!

The environment needs our help,
We must recycle all we can,
Old newspapers, even a pan.

Greener we must be,
We must kick litter into touch,
Then we will be green,
Healthy and clean.

Get out of your car,
And use the bus,
Less pollution for all of us!

Keep the water clean,
Free from any oil,
The animals would stay healthy,
And nothing would spoil.

Nathan Sweeney (10)
Our Lady's RC Primary School, Aspull

Litter

Litter, litter everywhere
People just don't listen, they just don't care.
We need to stand up and shout
'Get rid of those litter louts!'

Take your time, you need to think
Green bin, brown bin, black or pink?
But please don't drop it on the floor
We need to learn to recycle more.

Cardboard, glass, tins and plastic
Paper and foil, these are all fantastic!
So if we all put up a fight
We'll keep down that landfill site.

Jake Bithell (9)
Our Lady's RC Primary School, Aspull

Recycling!

Anyone can recycle,
It's really easy to do.
Glass, plastic,
Paper,
Even pop cans too.

Reduce, reuse, recycle.
To reduce you crush
It very small.
Don't drop it on the floor,
Don't, don't let it fall.

Reduce, reuse, recycle.
Reuse is when you've done a drawing wrong.
Turn it over!
And write a song.

Megan Leyland (10)
Our Lady's RC Primary School, Aspull

The Big Green Poetry Machine

There was a big green machine,
That loved to eat things,
So anything you see on the floor,
Please pick up and throw.

We love to keep our environment clean,
So we don't get any dirty disease,
Start to pick up more litter,
So we can recycle all the things.

Animals are nearly killed every day,
We need to save the day.
We can start by not cutting down the trees,
Animals don't like it,
So I ask you stop it.

Joshua Caldwell (9)
Our Lady's RC Primary School, Aspull

Litter

Litter, litter everywhere
Whoever throws it should take care,
Litter, litter down the street,
It does not look very neat.

There's a black bin,
A green bin,
A brown one too,
They love litter, they
Love you.

Reanna Landa (11)
Our Lady's RC Primary School, Aspull

Rainforests

We must protect flowers, plants and trees,
And we might see some honeybees.
Let the waterfalls run,
And don't fire a gun.
We can send money to help,
Even if it's for an animal or sea kelp.
Don't cut down trees,
And don't put litter in the seas!
Help protect rainforests!

Roanne Cox (9)
Our Lady's RC Primary School, Aspull

The Earth - Haiku

The Earth needs saving
Recycle plastic bottles
Less carbon footprint.

Patrick Jepson (10)
Our Lady's RC Primary School, Aspull

Environment

Recycle, recycle all of your tins,
Sort them out in the colourful bins.
Paper, plastic, metal and even glass,
Recycle at home or in your class.

Even though lights are nice and bright,
You don't need them on morning till night.
For the light, use the sun,
Saving energy can be lots of fun.

Jamie Smith (10)
Our Lady's RC Primary School, Aspull

Wild And Free

Lovely animals please take care,
Don't make coats out of animal fur,
Bears and tigers and pandas too,
Help save their food especially bamboo.

Keep their habitats safe and clean,
Take home your rubbish and don't be mean.
All the creatures on land and sea,
Deserve to be happy, wild and free.

Samuel Foster (9)
Our Lady's RC Primary School, Aspull

I Give You And You Give Me

I give you flowers,
You give me weeds.
I give you lots of food,
You give me no love.
I give you objects,
You give me dead logs.
I give you the world,
You give me a polluted world.

Connor Wilcox (7)
Our Lady's RC Primary School, Aspull

Give And Take

I give you nice food,
You give me dirty litter.
I give you healthy things,
You give animals in need.
I give you happy children,
You give me lots of pollution.
I give you clean air,
You give me factories that don't care.

Connor Smith (8)
Our Lady's RC Primary School, Aspull

Save All Animals

You take animals in your home, like dogs, cats and birds,
But others live on their own, like lions, tigers and bears.
Some are endangered, their homes, their lives destroyed,
For people who don't seem to care, for this, I am annoyed.
Just take some time to think about how nice our world could be,
Adopt an endangered animal and show you care like me.

Lauren Newton (9)
Our Lady's RC Primary School, Aspull

I Give You, You Give Me

I give you beautiful trees,
You give me not a nice world.
I give you the forest,
You give me weeds.
I give you melons,
You give me extinct things.
I give you beautiful birds,
You give me nothing.

Deanna Cullen (8)
Our Lady's RC Primary School, Aspull

Litter

Throwing litter is not fun
Neither is spitting out gum.
People who do this are dumb,
Throw your rubbish in the bin.
Spitting gum on the floor is a sin,
So don't be dim,
Be good and put it in the bin.

Martyn Parr (9)
Our Lady's RC Primary School, Aspull

Help Us

We must help the Earth,
Every little bit will help,
Just stick together!

Help the trees and plants,
Help the environment,
Help to save the Earth!

Zarah Tabrizi (10)
Our Lady's RC Primary School, Aspull

Helping The Environment

Recycle payer, recycle tin,
These should all go in your recycle bin.
Helping the environment is what we should do,
This is why you should recycle too.
It is not very hard to do it this way,
So let's all recycle day after day.

Joshua Fairhurst (10)
Our Lady's RC Primary School, Aspull

Give And Take

I give you colourful flowers,
You give me acid showers.
I give you wholemeal wheat,
You give me a dirty street.
I give you a great solution,
You give me lots of pollution.

Matthew Millard (7)
Our Lady's RC Primary School, Aspull

Do Your Bit!

Do your bit to save the world
Global warming have you heard?
Help clean up the dirty world,
So much pollution tut, tut, tut!
Help, time is running out
Global warming, pollution is swarming.

Thomas O'Brien (10)
Our Lady's RC Primary School, Aspull

Saving Our World

Don't make waste in a haste,
Or it'll leave the animals with an awful taste.

Please recycle,
And use your bicycle.

Help the people in the streets,
Give them homes,
Prevent their diseases.

Don't be bitter,
Pick up your litter,
Then it won't hurt the little critters.

The rainforest is precious,
Global warming is bad,
This is because of cars,
Which cause climate change.

To save our planet,
There is a solution,
Just cut down on our pollution.

If we want to stay on this world,
We will have to care.
So look after your town!

Conor George Mills (10)
Prospect Vale Primary School, Cheadle

Don't Drop Litter!

We all drop litter,
Because we're all bitter.
Throw everything in the bin,
Apart from paper and tin.
Recycle them as much as you can,
And leave them for the recycle man!

Iqra Hussain
Prospect Vale Primary School, Cheadle

How Would You Feel?

How would you feel?
If you had no food or water.
How would you feel?
If you had no home to go to.
How would you feel?
If you had no warm and safe place to be.
How would you feel?
If you had no clothes to wear.
How would you feel?
If you could not afford to go to school.
How would you feel?
If you had to work hard all day.
How would you feel?
If you had no toys.
How would you feel?
If you had no parents to love you.

I know how I would feel.
I would be sad and frightened.
I know how you would feel.
So let's all do something about it!

Henry Firmston (11)
Prospect Vale Primary School, Cheadle

Save The World

People are dying every day.
We need to stop war for the future, stop it for good!
We could help with only a penny,
That penny would help build schools and houses.
Please help stop poverty!
There are bins everywhere, so don't be a litterbug, save Earth!

Don't hunt or the rest of us will take the blame,
Animals are here for a reason, stop extinction!

Kieran O'Donnell-Davis (10)
Prospect Vale Primary School, Cheadle

Try Our Best

The weather has its own mind,
That you can never find,
Sometimes it needs a rest,
Then it's our turn to do our best,
The hailing wind,
Makes us frown.

We use cars to get around
Even though they help us,
Look at what I found,
They can be danger to your world,
Which is curled.

Trees help us breathe,
Paper comes from them,
Which helps us read.

Our world needs us
To try our best because
Now it needs a rest!

Sidrah Ahmed (10)
Prospect Vale Primary School, Cheadle

War

I think war should be a crime,
As it's fighting and shooting all the time.
All over the world is where it happens,
Everywhere being bombed.
It's always a reason that can be sorted out,
Without killing anyone.
But horrible people rule our world,
Who always resolve to killing.
Now this poem has come to an end,
But war goes back to the beginning.

Bethany Street (11)
Prospect Vale Primary School, Cheadle

The World!

The world all around us,
The flowers that surround us,
Its beauty is beyond comprehension,
This world is ours, in all directions.

Each one of us has a reason,
To destroy the wonderful seasons,
With songs of greed that we sing,
To perish the summer, winter, autumn and spring.

Who's to blame? Can they show?
Who's at fault? But we all know!
Let's look deep inside our hearts,
Blame ourselves - that's a start.

It's a big wide world and I'm so small,
Even when I stand, I'm not that tall.
The truth is said, what can you do, you're so strange?
But with me I know, the world can change!

Khadijah Ghaznavi (10)
Prospect Vale Primary School, Cheadle

Helping The Environment!

E veryone wants a cleaner world
N o one wants it dirty.
V ery few people help to keep it clean
I try my best to do my bit.
R ecycling is one thing I do
O r walking instead of driving.
N ot leaving the taps on, it wastes water
M aking sure the telly's switched off.
E veryone wants a cleaner world
N o one wants it dirty.
T oday it's your turn to help!

James Cottrell (8)
Prospect Vale Primary School, Cheadle

Where Did All The Animals Go?

It makes me sad to know,
In one hundred years or so,
They'll say, 'Where did all the animals go?'
'I wish I'd seen a panda or a polar bear,
Koala bears and turtles aren't to be found anywhere.'

It makes me angry to know,
That as human numbers grow,
We pollute the air, like we just don't care.
We chop down trees, that the monkeys need.
And in Japan there's no whaling ban.
Surely that's not fair!

It makes me glad to know,
That children want to show,
That they can make a difference,
And maybe with persistence,
The world will learn to grow.

Alexandra Argyle (10)
Prospect Vale Primary School, Cheadle

The Rainforest

From our heads to our toes
We love everything that grows.
Mankind is chopping down trees,
Bringing the rainforest to its knees.
Some animals live there, some don't
But this is no reason to take their home.
All the animals that die will go to Heaven in the sky.
If we don't stop chopping down,
It will soon be all flat ground.
No more homes for animals to live, just open space.
It's a disgrace!
Mankind.

Coby James Blackburn (10)
Prospect Vale Primary School, Cheadle

Let's Save The World

I am upset about poverty and the poor,
Could we give water, food, shelter and more?
Racism and name calling really annoys me,
We should stop it, can't everybody just be?
Everybody wastes things every day,
People who do not recycle should have to pay.
I just hate everything about pollution,
Walking to school is my solution.
I wish there was a cure for AIDS,
Couldn't we just make it fade?
There is a big problem with the homeless,
Couldn't we raise money and solve this big mess?
Animals and extinction is a very sad thing,
Why don't we stop all the killing?

Megan Banski-Munro (10)
Prospect Vale Primary School, Cheadle

Be Good, Be Green!

We all must recycle and never litter,
Please do this and don't be bitter,
Animals are dying of extinction from choking on junk.
Recycle, recycle, recycle!

Litter, please not,
This world's gonna get far too hot,
Our ozone layer is thinning,
Recycle, recycle, recycle!

We can all do this without a doubt,
Otherwise we will be left with nowt.
There is only one word you have to remember,
That's
Recycle, recycle, recycle!

Ria Louise Meredith (10)
Prospect Vale Primary School, Cheadle

The World - As We Know It

We know the world is dying,
But few people are trying,
To recycle, reuse, and reduce,
And stop their abuse.

It's time to start preventing what *we* do to it,
And start doing our bit,
To help pollution, poverty,
And treat the world properly.

We need to think about the people who live on the streets,
The colds they catch and the diseases they meet.
Animals and extinction, racism and war,
These are all examples of what others' lives have in store.
Treat our world with some respect!

Sophie Morgan (10)
Prospect Vale Primary School, Cheadle

To Save The Planet

The world is the place where we live
So if we want it to stay we've got to look after it.
The animals should live longer and we should recycle a bit,
So if we don't recycle the rubbish will go on the streets.
If we don't save the world we won't be here,
Neither will the plants.
We should also save people on the planet.
So let's give money to the poor and homeless,
And make the world a happy place for everyone and everything.

Scarlett Sinnett (8)
Prospect Vale Primary School, Cheadle

Untitled

I went to the lake the other day,
For goodness sake, what has happened to our lake?
It's covered in plastic of all shapes, and sizes,
Tyres and bikes and a mouldy old kite.
If only we could make this messy old lake be beautiful and clean,
Just how it should have been.
With hard work and education
We could make this lake an animal haven.
It just takes dedication!

Georgia Lee (10)
Prospect Vale Primary School, Cheadle

A Better World

We are all in a race,
To make the world a better place.
We have to stop the climate changing,
Let's get together and help with recycling.
Many animals face extinction,
Stop, stop, stop the pollution.
The rainforests have nearly all gone,
If we educate ourselves the race will be won.

Zayn Ali (10)
Prospect Vale Primary School, Cheadle

Our Earth

If you want this Earth to exist in another thousand years,
Then do your bit by shutting doors
And turning lights off when not being used.
Then one day you will see a world with no more tears.

Sally Crompton-Whittle (10)
Prospect Vale Primary School, Cheadle

Litter

Litter, litter everywhere,
Makes you think, do people care?
It's harmful to animals, children too,
Do the litterbugs not have a clue?
All it takes is for the human race,
To put it in its rightful place.
So listen up people, don't be a fool,
Use a bin and be really cool.

Lewis Griffiths (11)
Prospect Vale Primary School, Cheadle

My Homeless Life

H is for the home I had
O is for ordeal
M is for the money I beg for
E is for the endless time
L is for loneliness
E is for everything I dream of
S is for the street I live on
S is for a sad heart.

Alycia Anwar (8)
Prospect Vale Primary School, Cheadle

The Army

T hey try to be the best
H oping God is on their side.
E very mother worries!

A lways helping people who are in serious trouble
R emembering the dead
M aking a difference
Y et we still have wars.

Ben Cottrell (8)
Prospect Vale Primary School, Cheadle

A Little Love

Imagine a little dog sat all on its own
Waiting for a bit of love with no home,
Just looking at people staring.
Imagine that dog waiting to play, but no one is around to play.
He is really cute and sweet but there doesn't seem to be any
People around where he is.
He only wants a bit of love, can't we give a bit of love to abandoned dogs?
Please stop this happening.
Imagine a stray dog on the streets,
Imagine dog fights, dogs looking in a state.
Imagine a dog with one eye.
Fur nearly all gone, and it has fleas.
Imagine you being a dog and no one loved you, how would you feel?
Would you feel sad or would you feel lonely?
You wouldn't like it would you?
So when you see a dog on the streets or maybe even on your holidays,
Just think and remind yourself what it would be like.
Thank you, please stop this happening.

Mareesa Smith (9)
SS Aidan & Oswald RC Primary School, Royton

Be Greener

Be greener,
Be greener,
Make our world cleaner,
Everywhere we walk,
And everywhere we talk.
Recycle,
Recycle,
Maybe learn to cycle,
We need fresh air,
So drivers beware.
Lights out,
Lights out,
Always when it's bright out.
When you're out at work
Don't be an energy jerk.
Save trees
Save trees
Pretty, pretty please.
Don't waste paper,
Be a tree saver,
Off with the light
And everything will be alright.

Georgia Bradshaw (10)
SS Aidan & Oswald RC Primary School, Royton

Have You Heard The Word?

Have you heard the word?
We are polluting our big bad world.
Our rainforests are dying because we're not trying.
Stop using your car and we'll go far.
I'm in your face because the world should be a better place.
Use your bicycle and start to recycle.
Now hear my word.

Georgia Lowe (10)
SS Aidan & Oswald RC Primary School, Royton

The Green

The ozone layer's failing,
The weather's really changing.
With hurricanes and earthquakes,
And even tsunamis too.
Solar panels and wind farms,
Are helping energy last.
But while we are still tipping rubbish,
The ozone just won't last.
We breathe in dirty car fumes,
Each and every day.
And while our streets are littered,
The mice and rats will stay.
So we can all join in together,
And do our little bit.
Put paper, card, glass and tins,
In their designated bins,
And if you see someone dropping rubbish on our streets,
Tell them they need to be wise,
Or face a massive fine.

Matthew McQuillan (9)
SS Aidan & Oswald RC Primary School, Royton

Keep The World Clean

Recycle, recycle, recycle
And go to school on your bicycle.
Don't use a car that poisons the air.
It's better to walk and show that we care.
Give your bottles and cans to the recycle men,
Who will take them away so we can use them again.
If we don't recycle and reuse our waste
We won't make our world a better place.
So look after the planet and keep it clean.
The future's not orange, it's gotta be green.

Georgia McCombe (9)
SS Aidan & Oswald RC Primary School, Royton

Hunger

People are crying
People are crying
They don't have any food
They need food
They need food
Or they will die
Of hunger
Of hunger
Imagine us with no food.
Oh why is the world so sad?
People are crying with no food inside them
You should be grateful, be grateful,
Don't throw food away.
We could help by giving them food
Like bread and crisps
So that they don't die,
Don't die and give them fresh water.

Rosalie Berry (8)
SS Aidan & Oswald RC Primary School, Royton

Litter Is For Losers

Don't be a fool and follow this golden rule.
When you're walking down the street and litter is at your feet.
Do the right thing man
And put it in the trash can.
Make this country clean
And don't be selfish and mean.
Have some pride
And get on the right side.
Pick up litter
And don't be a quitter.
If everybody followed this rule
Our country would be clean and cool!

Ellen McLoughlin (10)
SS Aidan & Oswald RC Primary School, Royton

Care For The Environment

Don't litter
Put your rubbish in the bins
Packets, wrappers and tins
Recycle, recycle, recycle!
Do more good stuff
Plant flowers
Report crimes
Recycle, recycle, recycle!
Don't commit crimes
Put them behind
You'll get in trouble with the police
Recycle, recycle, recycle!
Graffiti, stabbings, crimes put them behind
Don't litter, don't be bitter, recycle
And help the world be clean.

Bethany Williamson (9)
SS Aidan & Oswald RC Primary School, Royton

Think Of The Future

Will politicians try to save face,
And make the world a better place.
Rid the land of all pollution,
If only we could find a solution?
Rainforests becoming less and less,
Oh dear, the world is such a mess.
If someone introduced a law,
Banning the world from going to war.
World poverty at an end,
Grateful for all donations you send.
Recycle and don't throw away,
Do something positive, we hear you say.
Small changes help in a big way,
Think of the children - do something today.

Jack Dugdale (10)
SS Aidan & Oswald RC Primary School, Royton

Recycling Poem

Black box, wheelie bin,
Which one does the glass go in?
Plastic bottle, tinfoil trays
Can all be recycled, Daddy says.

All our rubbish left lying around
Can be used again as it has been found.
Who would have thought that an old shoebox
Could now be a cosy bed for my toy fox?

So please go on and give it a try
Recycle, recycle and you'll see why.
It's not all rubbish and it's not all waste
Don't throw things in haste.
See if you can make use of rubbish, it's not wrong,
And help our planet to keep growing strong.

Emma Atkinson (9)
SS Aidan & Oswald RC Primary School, Royton

Four Bins

Four bins in a line
Standing tall looking fine.

Black, green, brown and blue
Waiting for recycling for me and you.

They hold cans, glass and paper and card
Paper and grass, it's not that hard.

Don't leave rubbish on the floor
Kick your carbon footprint and try to score.

We are saving the world you know
Keep your rubbish at an all-time low.

Don't make the world grey,
Make it glow!

Nicholas Connor (9)
SS Aidan & Oswald RC Primary School, Royton

The Environment

The environment is very green.
But we still need to be seen.
But we won't if you don't recycle,
And please don't forget to recycle.
When you can also cycle to school.
Also let's not forget the litter,
Take it to the bin.
As you're committing a great sin
Danger is killing our planet.
If you litter get ready to panic
Give your empty cans to the can man
Reuse your paper,
If you do then get ready to shout,
Recycle, recycle, recycle.

Sophie Lee (9)
SS Aidan & Oswald RC Primary School, Royton

Stop It!

Walk to school
Don't smoke
It's poisoning the world
What's wrong
With people?
Killing and fighting
People polluting
Get food from near
Or you release greenhouse gases.
Stop it!
You're destroying
Polluting our world
We only have one world!

Kieran Liam McDonough (8)
SS Aidan & Oswald RC Primary School, Royton

Animals In Extinction

Animals, animals, animals
Some are mammals
Some are camels
They are nearly in extinction
They are nearly in fiction
They dance about
They prance about
Some have spots
Some have dots
Some have very crinkly skin
Some have very prickly skin
They are nearly in extinction
They are nearly in fiction.

Tanya Field (10)
SS Aidan & Oswald RC Primary School, Royton

Komodo Dragon

Is there any peace here
On this lone desolate island?
All my family and friends are dead,
From men and women.

Komodo is endangered,
We'd do anything if you'd stop.
Each day and night we dream 'Would it stop?'
But we find it won't.

Soon I too shall get shot,
Please help us,
We'd do anything.
If you'd stop shooting.

Patrick Cooke (9)
SS Aidan & Oswald RC Primary School, Royton

Just Recycle

Help keep our environment green,
We can all do this work as a team.
Let's all remember to recycle your waste,
Paper, bottles, tin cans too.
You can help, it's down to you.
Never throw your litter on the floor,
Help your environment even more.
Remember to save electricity to turn your lights off,
It's down to you.
Spread the word by telling another,
Tell your sister and your brother,
It's down to you.

Mia Taurasi (9)
SS Aidan & Oswald RC Primary School, Royton

Litter, Litter, Everywhere

Litter, litter, everywhere, put it in the bin over there.
If you leave it on the floor, it will pile up more and more.
It would smell and attract some mice,
That would not be very nice.
It's maybe unsafe for me and you,
It could smell like we're down the loo.
Our streets should be nice and clean,
Our environment needs to be green.
So please don't be a litterbug,
Give the environment a great big hug.
Put your litter in the bin,
And walk away with a great big grin.

Niall Heap (10)
SS Aidan & Oswald RC Primary School, Royton

I Saw A Recycling Box

I saw a recycling box.
I saw green bottles.
I saw some old tins waiting to be reused.
I saw a green bin.
I saw old grass trimmings.
I saw plastic bottles in a recycling bin.
I saw a black bin.
I saw a recycling symbol.
I saw a sign that read 'Recycle Oldham'
I saw a sickening thing.
I'll tell you what it was,
Someone was out shopping with at least a dozen new plastic bags.

Rachel Rajkovic (9)
SS Aidan & Oswald RC Primary School, Royton

Let's All Be Green

Let's all be green,
Walking to school is green and makes you lean,
Litter is bad, litter is mean,
Let's all be green,
Let's all be green,
It's very cool and don't be a fool,
Stop cutting down our trees, we'll have no leaves,
Let's all be green,
Let's all be green,
Turn off your light and you'll be bright,
Reuse your paper and you'll be a saver.
Let's all be green.

Oliver Andrew Stewart (9)
SS Aidan & Oswald RC Primary School, Royton

Save The World

I had a dream,
That humans changed their minds.
The bears were free,
The water was clean and there were no wars.
But when I woke up,
I found that it was not true.
The bears were back in cages,
And the water was as dark as mud,
And World War III was going on.
It was so sad to find that it was just a dream.
So stop destroying the world and start to save it.

Bethany Smith (9)
SS Aidan & Oswald RC Primary School, Royton

Environment Of The World

Seeing lots of litter
On the streets floating about
Makes me bitter
And want to shout!

It doesn't take much
To do a good deed
Just pop your rubbish in the right bin
They like to have a feed!

The environment need us now and forever
Doing your bit may help improve the weather.

Samuel Kinsella (9)
SS Aidan & Oswald RC Primary School, Royton

Bins, Bins, Lots Of Bins

A bin for food! Food that you've left
When you're not in the mood.

A bin for paper, because paper isn't free,
To make that paper they've chopped down a tree.

A bin for bottles made of glass
Into the recycling they go with a smash!

It's good to recycle, it keeps the environment green.
That's what we are taught
And that's what I've seen.

Jack Smith (9)
SS Aidan & Oswald RC Primary School, Royton

Save The Environment

To save the environment what can you do?
Recycle your rubbish, plastic, cans and paper too.

Don't drop litter or spit your gum
If we work together we can make it more fun.

Leave nature to nature, wildlife to reset
There are all kinds of ways you'll be doing your best.

So everyone start listening, woman, man, boy and girl,
Let's all work together
To start saving our world.

Alex Summerscales (9)
SS Aidan & Oswald RC Primary School, Royton

Litter

Litter in the park
Light colours and dark
Dried up on the beach.
Things like yucky peach
Sometimes people recycle
Then they can ride and cycle.
Why is the world so bad?
People are getting sad.
Wrapping paper, chocolate bars.
Sweety wrappers and dried up stars.

Aimee Elizabeth Canny (7)
SS Aidan & Oswald RC Primary School, Royton

Recycle!

I pick up rubbish from the floor,
I do this to impress Mrs Moore.
I kick the trash up from the lift,
I make the people shift.
I try my best to keep the world green,
This is what they've never seen,
An Earth that is so clean!
I think we should all keep Britain tidy,
So wake up people and don't be lazy.
Recycle, recycle, recycle and ride your bicycle.

Shah Al-Maruf (9)
SS Aidan & Oswald RC Primary School, Royton

I Saw

I saw a monkey recycling a bottle
I saw a tiger planting a tree
I saw a parrot putting paper in the compost bin
I saw a worm eating the compost that the parrot put in
I saw, I saw, I saw.
I saw a lion turning off a light
I saw a gorilla reusing his bags
I saw a lizard recycling a banana
I saw a komodo dragon riding a bike to school
I saw, I saw, I saw.

Joseph Kershaw (9)
SS Aidan & Oswald RC Primary School, Royton

Recycling Poem

Every week we fill our bins,
Green bins, brown bins, blue an' black.

Green ones full of fresh cut grass
And brown ones full of broken glass.

Out they wheel on a Wednesday night,
Ready for the waste paper site.

All the waste is recycled back,
To help the planet's plants grow back.

Josh Bridges (9)
SS Aidan & Oswald RC Primary School, Royton

Freedom

I had a dream
The animals were free
That's how it would be
That's how it should be
That's how we want it
Except for some few
Those few hunt them down
Not how we want it
How can we stop it?

Aaron Davies (9)
SS Aidan & Oswald RC Primary School, Royton

Water

Water is dirty.
People are dying from dirty water to thirst.
We have clean and fresh water but they don't.
We only have to go the tap but they have to walk miles for water.
We have people to make water clean,
But they don't have people to make water clean.
Remember you have benefits like clean water
And you never will thirst but they just might.
When you take a drink, just stop and think.

Barney Franklin (8)
SS Aidan & Oswald RC Primary School, Royton

Environment Lives

Environment, environment, good for the world
If you did not help the environment
Toxic waste would cover the world.
So recycle all your things you don't want.

Bailey Lynch (9)
SS Aidan & Oswald RC Primary School, Royton

The World

The world is a great place
Because you get to live, play with your friends
And have a great time,
But if you litter or if you're cutting down trees,
Or even not recycling,
The littliest thing could end the world.
So try your best not to litter or cut down trees
Or kill animals, or not recycle.
So stop and think about what you are doing.

Courtney Coverley (10)
SS Aidan & Oswald RC Primary School, Royton

Dream Come True

Every night I dream that all animals from all countries
Would be let free out into safe worlds.
Don't let people kill animals.
Please let's make a stop to this now.
It is so easy.
There are dogs crying out there, and other animals.
Give some money to owners so they can pay for better things for them.
Go on please give one pound.

Dana Tiegan Parry (9)
SS Aidan & Oswald RC Primary School, Royton

Untitled

I drank my Coca-Cola, threw the bottle in the recycle bin.
So the council take it away to use it again, and again and again.
I love to recycle, I will never ever stop
But people who don't recycle will have to clean it with a mop.

Ross Doolan (9)
SS Aidan & Oswald RC Primary School, Royton

Stop Pollution

Pollution is bad, it's everywhere.
Gas fumes make poison.
Stop! We need to clear the air.
Animals are dying all around.
Stop! We need to hear their sound.
People throw litter onto the ground
Stop! We need to turn it around.
What can be done, have you a clue?
Stop! It's easy, it starts with you!

Thomas Barnes (7)
SS Aidan & Oswald RC Primary School, Royton

Litter

I look around and what do I see?
Lots of litter all around me.
If only people would take a care,
Throw the litter in the bins that are everywhere.

It's up to us to keep the world clean,
So next time you're out, don't be mean,
Take your litter home if you can't find a bin,
Make it a cleaner place for us all to live in.

Oliver Gartside (11)
SS Aidan & Oswald RC Primary School, Royton

Be Green

If you recycle, you'll make our world a better place.
If we don't litter, it won't be a disgrace.
Be green, be green.
It will make everything clean.
Recycle plastic, tins, cardboard and other things.
Grass and glass both go in bins,
Everything you don't want, like cardboard and tins,
Keep your environment green.

Benjamin James Cooper (9)
SS Aidan & Oswald RC Primary School, Royton

The Pollution

Pollution is smelly fumes
And is disgusting and unhealthy.
Pollution is spreading everywhere,
Pick up the rubbish.
Animals are getting killed.
We're not making the world a better place.
The smoke is not good.
The animals don't want to die.

Abby Winnard (7)
SS Aidan & Oswald RC Primary School, Royton

Making The World A Better Place

What can we do about litter? It makes me feel all bitter.
We need to cut down on how much we use our cars.
With the money we spend on petrol we could probably go to Mars.
Recycling rules, littering drools.
Help make this world a better place.
So we can save the human race.

Michael Hadfield (9)
SS Aidan & Oswald RC Primary School, Royton

Stop The Wars

Stop the war right now,
Please stop the war right now,
Please make the big difference for everybody's life
And save people's lives and save children's lives and babies' lives
And stop fighting the wars right now
Or your family can get hurt or killed from the wars.
Someone please stop it now or you're going to be killed.
Save yourself, your family and the world.

Abigail Jane Harris (8)
SS Aidan & Oswald RC Primary School, Royton

Recycle

This is my message to you.
The environment needs you;
Tell your family, tell your friends.
Green is mean, green is keen.
Green is a recycling machine.
Recycle bottles, recycle cans,
Recycle pots, recycle pans.
Remember anything goes!

Mia White (9)
SS Aidan & Oswald RC Primary School, Royton

Water

If we waste water we should give poor people water.
Poor people have dirty water
They have to walk with buckets up and down the streets
Collecting dirty water they have to drink.
How would you feel if you were like them,
Lonely, sad, crying, unhappy?

Ethan Cadd (8)
SS Aidan & Oswald RC Primary School, Royton

Pouring Rain

People walking through the pouring rain,
People trying to drive to work.
But we are very lucky, we have cars, buses, trains, motorbikes and
lots of vehicles
So that we can get through the pouring rain,
So that we can get through the rain without getting wet,
And we also have coats, hats, scarves and umbrellas,
So be grateful for what we have got in our world.

Charlotte Emerson (9)
SS Aidan & Oswald RC Primary School, Royton

Litter, Never Litter

Litter, never litter
Litter, litter is so mean, why can't you keep stuff clean.
Garbage, garbage is so vile, if there was none, everyone would
smile.
Pollute, pollute is so bad, if there was clear, no one would be mad.
Now, now there is no more, glass will not make my feet sore.
Litter, litter is so mean, why can't you keep stuff clean.
Litter, never litter.

Joshua Ferguson (9)
SS Aidan & Oswald RC Primary School, Royton

Being Green

Being green saves energy,
Being green is clean,
Being green saves pollution,
Being green helps the planet,
Being green helps the air,
Being green is fun.

Lucas Dawson (9)
SS Aidan & Oswald RC Primary School, Royton

Animals

The snow bears love the snow
Soon they will have nowhere to go.
The ice is melting with global warming
The poor bears are falling.
We could stop if we cared
So why don't we say a prayer?
They might hurt you but they don't know what they do
So please don't shoot.

Dean Wright (8)
SS Aidan & Oswald RC Primary School, Royton

Pollution

Pollution is everywhere in the city.
Oceans full of plastic bottles and boxes of litter in the street,
Litter in the ocean and wherever you stand or sit,
Litter in your house, litter everywhere,
Terrible things are happening everywhere,
So come on Britain, let's stop and think,
To make this planet a better place for all.

Ethan Chiappe (7)
SS Aidan & Oswald RC Primary School, Royton

Saved The World

I had a dream:
The humans changed their minds,
They let out the bears from the zoo,
They stopped catching fish and eating them.
The world could be made better.
Don't eat fish, don't catch dolphins
And I wish, I wish, I wish, you don't eat fish!

Amber Taljard (9)
SS Aidan & Oswald RC Primary School, Royton

Pollution

Pollution is a dirty fume made by us.
It's made in the air and on the sea.
People just throw their litter so we have to do something about it.
Planes spray out smoke and make pollution in the air.
Boats chuck oil out into the sea.
Animals are dying,
But wherever you go remember pollution is made by us.

Jake Wilson (7)
SS Aidan & Oswald RC Primary School, Royton

Recycle Every Day

Recycle, recycle we must recycle.
Pollution is not the real solution.
Compost, compost we must make compost.
Our world is evolving but it started dissolving.
Green, green, glorious green.
Our world is dying, we must stop buying.
Do it now, do it now and save our world.

Emily Sheppard (9)
SS Aidan & Oswald RC Primary School, Royton

Being Green

If you want to be green,
You have to be clean.

Don't just throw it in the bin,
'Cause it would be a real sad sin.

Paper, cans, tins and wood,
Recycling them does so much good.

Ben Robert Francis Partington (9)
SS Aidan & Oswald RC Primary School, Royton

Green

I want to keep the world very clean
Not the colours that look so mean.
Recycle, recycle everything you can
From top to bottom everywhere you can.

I want to keep our world very clean
So we all have to be a little bit green.

Jennifer Weir (9)
SS Aidan & Oswald RC Primary School, Royton

Recycle Madness

Recycling boxes banging.
Tins and glasses clattering
Cans, bottles banging,
Paper and card scrunching
To the recycling bank all must go
On for evermore.

George Lord (10)
SS Aidan & Oswald RC Primary School, Royton

Recycle, Recycle, Recycle

Put your waste paper and rubbish in bins,
Newspapers, bottles, boxes and tins.
Keep the streets clean,
For all to be seen.
The more we recycle, the better it will be.
The streets will be cleaner, for all to see.

Nicola Webb (9)
SS Aidan & Oswald RC Primary School, Royton

Litter Poem

Look at all this litter
And waste, it's quite disgusting
Isn't it Michael?
Let's pick it all up and take it home
Then put it in our dustbins to recycle.

Ethan Cartwright (9)
SS Aidan & Oswald RC Primary School, Royton

Recycle

Don't be lazy, show you care
By doing your share on our environment.
Recycle, recycle, recycle
To keep our world looking good, please recycle if you could.
Keep the litter off the ground and use all the bins you see around.

Brandon Seale (9)
SS Aidan & Oswald RC Primary School, Royton

The Environment

The environment is very cool, that's why we're learning it at school.
I find it really fun and I agree littering should not be done.
I do what I can to save the Earth because it is the place of my birth.
I don't want to live on Venus or Mars
So stop polluting it with your cars!

Courtney Mills (9)
SS Aidan & Oswald RC Primary School, Royton

Our Earth

O is for ozone that's getting thin, if we cut our emissions our Earth can win.
U is for useful things that you can do with your waste, but time's running out so we must make haste.
R is for rubbish that we can reuse, please put it in your recycling refuse.

E is for energy, that's depleting fast, so turn down your electric and your gas.
A is for air that we need to be pure, so don't drive your car if you're not going far.
R is for recycling which we all can do, if we do this we will have a breakthrough.
T is for treasure which is our Earth, if we all work together there will be much mirth.
H is for hope for our lovely world, don't let it go, you have been told.

Leah Hollie Reid (8)
St John's CE Primary School, Heaton Mersey

Stop Pollution

If you want to be happy and fitter,
Go out and pick up some litter.
Stop pollution,
Do some more,
Help the homeless,
Save the poor!
Don't go in the car.
Go on your bicycle
Don't drop paper
Remember *recycle!*
Remember, remember, don't yelp
Remember, remember, you can help!

Natalie Murray (8)
St John's CE Primary School, Heaton Mersey

Keep It Clean

Keep our world clean
Keep our world tidy
Keep our world a beautiful place
Don't make a mess
Don't drop litter
Don't buy lots of food you can't eat
Recycle your plastic bottles and cans
Also your paper and cardboard boxes
Please help us to save our planet.

Grace Norcross (7)
St John's CE Primary School, Heaton Mersey

Don't Be Mean!

Don't be mean, keep it clean
Look after the world
And make it gleam.
Put your bottles in the recycling bin
Don't throw away your plastics, it's a sin.
Ride your bike, don't go in a car
Save in petrol and you will get a gold star.
Give your old clothes to the charity shop
The things you can do, just don't stop.

Alexandra Jordan Fox Graham (8)
St John's CE Primary School, Heaton Mersey

Being Green

Being green isn't so mean,
Being green is just clean,
Being green is cool to be seen,
Being green, join my team.

Helena Lucy Turley (9)
St John's CE Primary School, Heaton Mersey

Green, Green, Green

Green, green, green, makes the world not mean, mean, mean.
If you walk, walk, walk, you can talk, talk, talk.
If you're in a war, war, war, you will break the law, law, law.
Earth, Earth, Earth is worth, worth, worth everything.
Cycle, cycle, cycle, make sure you *recycle!*

Maya Nelson (8)
St John's CE Primary School, Heaton Mersey

Recycle Now

Recycle now, recycle now
Don't leave the world a disgrace
Recycle now, recycle now
Make the world a cleaner place.

Lily Ashbrook (7)
St John's CE Primary School, Heaton Mersey

Save Our World

S ounds of 'Help the world' go, go, go, no time to waste.
A car makes a lot of pollution, walk, walk!
V ery often white Bengal tigers are sadly dying,
E very day tigers are being shot by humans.

T he world is dying
H elp us all
E very year global warming destroys a bit of ice.

W hat matters more, us or the world?
O ur community lies in your hands
R euse, reduce, recycle
L et us survive!
D o good.

Aaron Nelson (8)
St Thomas' CE Primary School, Kendal

Recycling

Recycling is the best!

Even though it is a pest!

Blue box is for newspapers
That we read every day
Always recycle them
Don't throw them away.

Blue is for glass, cans and tins
So put them in here
Never in the grey bins.

When we tidy the garden
We use the green bin
Put grass cuttings, weeds
And all sorts of greens in.

Try to keep the grey bins very light
Don't put lots of rubbish in
As it ends up in a landfill site.

Be seen to be green
Keep our world clean!

Megan Harrington (8)
St Thomas' CE Primary School, Kendal

Saving The Earth

Do not litter and
Do not waste.
If you litter and if you waste, it will destroy your happy face!
If you chuck rubbish on the floor it will destroy the Earth more and more.
If you see someone putting paper in the bin
Tell them to get it *out again!*

Jamie Cribbens (9)
St Thomas' CE Primary School, Kendal

Help Save The Environment - Reuse

Recycle, reduce and reuse
You'd better never cruise.
Instead you should look in the bins
Recycle things and don't waste tins.
The polar bears' ice will melt,
While you make some felt
The atmosphere is a blanket of air
It's something the world has to share
Landfill sites are full to the top
This is something we've got to stop.

Sophie Walton (8)
St Thomas' CE Primary School, Kendal

Pollution

I have a solution to stop pollution
Recycling is a great sensation
To make the environment good for you
Only use cars when you need to.

Hannah Wood (8)
St Thomas' CE Primary School, Kendal

Recycling Will Do Us Good

What is killing our world?

P ollution is killing our world.
O ur fault that pollution is coming.
L itter is part of this.
L andfill is part of this too.
U nder these circumstances, global warming will erupt.
T omorrow is another day, we can start from then.
I t is invading our world.
O ur job is to stop it.
N ot likely to be stopped.

What can we do about it?

R ecycling will do us good.
E nergy can be saved.
C hange the world today.
Y our bit could be the difference.
C ans, glass, paper and cardboard.
L itter ties our world in knots, we must untie them.
E veryone can do their bit.

Connor Kilcullen (11)
St Winifred's RC Primary School, Heaton Mersey

Pollution Is Killing Us

P ollution killing the Earth
O zone has been destroyed by us
L itter has been thrown on the floor
L itter has partially destroyed us
U nder this circumstance we could all die
T o know if we are going to live, we will stop littering
I s there any way to stop the people?
O ver the years we have treated the world very bad,
N ever drop litter again.

Michael Dolan (11)
St Winifred's RC Primary School, Heaton Mersey

Pollution Vs Recycle Boy

Pollution is everywhere
He will always be watching you
Doing his very best to destroy our world
He smiles while the world slowly dies.

His smell is ghastly
You inhale his fumes anywhere and everywhere
Through cans, through power plants and even your litter
Do we really stand a chance?

But we have a comeback
Recycle Boy is here
A boy that is all rubbish
That you have recycled
By helping Recycle Boy
You are helping your planet
We still stand a chance
The fight is on.

Sean Sloane (10)
St Winifred's RC Primary School, Heaton Mersey

Do We Care?

Look at our world
All wretched and destroyed,
We're destroying everything there is.
Do we not care?
Walking through the strangling litter,
And sometimes I ask myself,
All these inventions, were they made to show off?
To show that we are clever?
So do we care about the environment?
So, no matter how flashy your Lamborghini,
You have to make a change, to stop landfills,
Acid rain and death, to live in a safe world and to make a difference.

Joseph Hayward (10)
St Winifred's RC Primary School, Heaton Mersey

A Destroyed World To Be Changed

Save the world from pollution and smoke
Our world needs help from you
Foggy skies and rain like tears, help! Help!
Make a difference and help the ozone layer
Stick to three rules and you can help
The rules are reduce, reuse, recycle
Help the putrid air
Get out of the car and walk to school
Because a change makes a difference
For the world to survive.

Charlotte Lambe (10)
St Winifred's RC Primary School, Heaton Mersey

Pollution

P oor amount of people recycling
O zone layer is being destroyed
L ook at our world
L andfills everywhere
U nmanageable amounts of litter
T oxic waste and a devastating amount of factories
I can help, you can help, we can all save the world
O verfilled landfills
N ow our world is destroyed.

Monica Hughes (10)
St Winifred's RC Primary School, Heaton Mersey

Global Warming

Global warming is very bad
It's making our Earth very sad.
It is happening so fast,
Our Earth won't last.
Our climate has changed
It's so sad.
We have to act right now
Or we will have no world.
That's how bad global warming is.

Daniel O'Neill (10)
St Winifred's RC Primary School, Heaton Mersey

Reduce, Reuse, Recycle

R ecycle our wasteful paper
E nd our Earth being polluted
C hange other people's lives
Y ou can do it, we all can
C hange the world
L earning to recycle can pass through families
E asy to recycle.

Reduce, reuse, recycle.

John Joseph Patrick Roberts (10)
St Winifred's RC Primary School, Heaton Mersey

Being Homeless

B abies being left all alone on the street to die,
Nobody to hear their cries and see their tears, all alone for evermore
E ating rubbish from out of the bins, nothing else to eat and no one to hear them on the streets
I ll and sick on the streets
N o mum and dad there to care, people say it's not fair
G rowling stomachs, can't go on, got to rest for ever and ever

H ungry and tired, can't go on, there is no hope for them now
O ut of their homes, no one to care, they don't want to go on so let them rest in peace
M ost parents out there care for their children but some don't care at all
E ach of us need to help to chase children's tears away
L ove and care are not there for children out there
E arly each morning they open their eyes to find no mum there in sight
S ad and cold, they lie and rest
S o we need to pull together and fight for them to have a better life in the future.

Hannah Bostock & Olivia Lawson (10)
The Meadows Primary School, Madeley Heath

Destroying Nature

Can't we stop cutting down trees?
Destroying animals' habitats is our crime.
Trees give us oxygen,
Too many forests are burning.
We're losing precious nature,
Ancient oak and woodlands disappear,
Without forests and trees, we wouldn't be here.

Joe Minshall (10) & James Bosson (9)
The Meadows Primary School, Madeley Heath

Rainforests!

R ainforests are being destroyed
A nimals are being killed
I nsects are losing life companions
N ot many people care about the environment!
F orest fires killing all!
O xygen is becoming scarce
R uining all of the people's lives
E xtinction happening too often, not always able to save
S uffering greatly for humans' pleasure
T rees burning, being cut down
S o, what can we do to save the rainforests?

Rebecca Louise Boult (10)
The Meadows Primary School, Madeley Heath

Rainforests

R edwood trees are dying, they do have feelings too you know
A ncient ruins are ruins no more, just a pile of stone and rock
I f you were cut down and killed, how would you feel?
N othing will be left, unless we save the trees and plants
F oliage is being lost, habitats of sweet animals
O rang-utans swing, but what will they swing on soon?
R hinos and tigers, pandas and monkeys, they will be soon gone
E ating seems easy to us, but what will the animals eat?
S kins of animals are being sold, animals of the forest
T rees breathe out oxygen and breathe in CO_2
S oon all of this will be gone, there will be nothing left.

Olivia Burton, Katie Smith & Scarlett Moore (10)
The Meadows Primary School, Madeley Heath

War

Hard ships sink
Blood appears.
Bombs explode
Ships overload
People fear.

Tanks go bang
Soldiers suffer
Children die
Parents cry
War gets tougher.

Jake Magee (10)
The Meadows Primary School, Madeley Heath

Rainforest

R oots suffering
A nimals evacuating
I nsects flying
N obody helping
F orests burning
O xygen lacking
R odents breeding
E ngine noises, pollution
S torms brewing
T rees dying.

Jack Sanders, Adam Heath (10) & Charlotte Fowler (9)
The Meadows Primary School, Madeley Heath

Recycle

R ecycle all your waste
E arth will be better off for it
C ompost bins are great for uncooked food
Y oghurt pots make fab kids toys
C leaner streets are best for all
L andfills will become less full
I nternationally this will help
N ever worry about little rats
G ood feelings all round!

Harriet Moore (10) & Lauren Greaves (11)
The Meadows Primary School, Madeley Heath

Destroying Nature

Animals are dying,
Newts, insects, tigers too
Gorillas becoming extinct,
Axes chopping forests down,
Wildlife hunted and killed,
We are destroying *nature*.

Daniel Fox (9)
The Meadows Primary School, Madeley Heath

War

War is death and no fun,
War is fighting, blood and loss.
War changes the lives of soldiers and families,
War is pointless,
Why, oh why?

George Jones (10)
The Meadows Primary School, Madeley Heath

War

War should be stopped,
Children die and land's destroyed.
Bombs blast, children terrified,
Animals are in danger,
People dying all around.

Brandon Matthews & Sam Cooper (9)
The Meadows Primary School, Madeley Heath

There's Litter Everywhere!

There's litter everywhere,
I can see a plastic bottle over there.
If you see some litter,
Put it in the bin, everywhere will glitter,
If we recycle soon,
We could help Earth by tomorrow afternoon.
Animals get stuck and killed by plastic,
Or even elastic!
We can save our Earth in many ways,
Just be patient, it'll take a few days.
If we act fast,
We could be called the heroes from the past!

Heather Louise Whincup (10)
Wimboldsley Primary School, Middlewich

Animals Of The Rainforest

In the trees swing the chimpanzees,
Chasing the bats are the wild cats,
Squawking parrots, make a riot,
Underneath the logs sit the frogs,
Alongside the lakes slither the snakes,
In the leaves sit the monkeys,
Watching the birds are the lizards.
Save the rainforests of the world!

Amy Ford (10)
Wimboldsley Primary School, Middlewich

Save Our Rainforest

Chopping too many rainforests down should not be allowed,
But for some reason the workmen are ridiculously proud.
We should be saving our trees,
In order to save our beloved chimpanzees.
Save our animals, this destruction must stop,
And don't let the size of the rainforest drop.
Our lives depend on it and the future of mankind,
We all must try together, until the end of time.

Ella Ross (10)
Wimboldsley Primary School, Middlewich

Where Will The Tiger Be?

Our world is full of eco,
It is full of green
Will our world remain like this?
Never! Unless we keep it clean:
The atom bomb,
Nuclear power,
Global warming,
Carbon and ozone,
These will all kill the planet.
Cars make terrible fumes,
Does this mean our Earth is doomed?
Try a bike or take a walk
If this carries on
Where will the tiger be? - gone!
Where will the whale be? - gone!
Where will the snow leopard be? - gone!
Where will the elephant be? - gone!
Whatever we do to the Earth,
We do to ourselves.

Owen Dowling (8)
Woodfall Primary School, Little Neston

Our Ruined World

Trees falling in the river,
Animals running away,
Eagles squeaking and leopards running,
Leaves turning grey.

Rivers overflowing,
Humans pushing it too far,
Ice caps melting,
The Earth begins to scar.

The temperature is getting hotter,
This is not good news,
Climate change disease and war,
We are losing all our zoos.

Factories pumping and pollution,
The air gets full of smoke,
We need to solve this problem now,
Everybody chokes!

Lucas Saulnier (9)
Woodfall Primary School, Little Neston

Ruined Rainforest

Fallen trees in rivers
Water all around,
Animals getting angry
Listening to the sounds.

Ice caps slowly melting
Causing lots of rain,
Because of all the people
It'll never be the same.

Rhinos are endangered
So are all the trees,
Fish are slowly dying
In the bubbling seas.

Cars chugging all around
Causing some pollution,
People are thinking
What is the solution?

Samuel James Hannah (10)
Woodfall Primary School, Little Neston

Our Precious Planet

Our world is green with eco, but we can't keep it up,
Animals that are endangered could get really stuck.
Stop going in the car, it causes lots of fumes,
Think about your planet or it will be doomed.

Our world is green with eco, we're getting better each time,
But if we're not that careful the sun will not shine.
We can see lots of litter on most of the streets,
But if we're not that careful we won't hear those tweets.

Our world is green with eco, we are nearly there,
This shouldn't have happened in the first place, because we really care.
And because of all the factories there is lots of smoke,
We need to cut this down or surely we'll choke.

So there we have it, a planet that's all green,
So never, never ever, ever be so mean.

Amelia Johnston (10)
Woodfall Primary School, Little Neston

Fragile World

Litter is bitter, swirling all around.
Animals choking on litter on the ground.
You can help save some animals if you don't drop litter.
You never know you could save a cat or a bat,
Or maybe a dog or a hog,
There's another way that you can help,
Go by foot instead of driving around in a car.
The world is sadly dying,
So if we want to keep it green, we'll have to keep it clean.
The world won't mind what you do to the environment,
Just as long as it's kind.
Try saving electricity, then you would save polar bears.
Think about these things and show that you care.

Grace Collinson (8)
Woodfall Primary School, Little Neston

Young Writers Information

We hope you have enjoyed reading this book - and that you will continue to enjoy it in the coming years.

If you like reading and writing poetry drop us a line, or give us a call, and we'll send you a free information pack.

Alternatively if you would like to order further copies of this book or any of our other titles, then please give us a call or log onto our website at www.youngwriters.co.uk

Young Writers Information
Remus House
Coltsfoot Drive
Peterborough
PE2 9JX
(01733) 890066